Tours FOR FREE™
COLORADO

Happy Touring!

Every effort has been made to insure the completeness and accuracy of all information in this book. However, the information in this book is subject to change at the discretion of the tour operators. It is recommended that you always call ahead when planning tours. Logos, packaging and photographs contained in this edition are either the trademark or copyright of the business that operates the tour. No compensation has been made to the publisher for inclusion of the tours in this book. It was the goal of the publisher to include as many free tours in the Colorado area as possible. Inclusion or exclusion of a tour does not imply any editorial or critical statement about any tour.

BentLight Media
© 2003 BentLight Media Inc.

Contact:
BentLight Media Inc. 637 S. Broadway B pmb 334 Boulder, CO 80305
Phone: 303.543.8532 • Toll Free: 888.851.5778
www.ToursForFree.com

Printed in the United States of America

ISBN: 1-893722-04-X

Library of Congress Cataloging-in-Publication Data Jill, Jodi

Tours For Free Colorado
1. Colorado - Tours - Handbooks, manuals, etc. 2. Tour guides (Manuals)
3. Manufacturing industries - United States - Directories. 4. Industries - United States - Directories.

Visual Engineering: Mercury Design Group - www.MercuryDG.com
Printer: Johnson Printing, Boulder, Colorado

Tours For Free Colorado is available at discount rates for educational, promotional, corporate gift packages and school fundraisers. Please contact the publisher at info@toursforfree.com or at the address and phone number above.

Printed on Recycled Paper

DENVER METRO

NORTHEAST

SOUTHEAST

SOUTHWEST

NORTHWEST

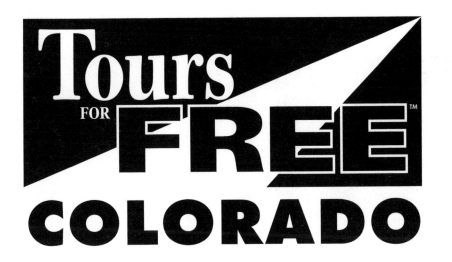

Tours FOR **FREE**™

COLORADO

This book is dedicated to every Coloradoan. Starting with the natives and pioneers who first saw the precious frontier, the people who cherish living in the Centennial state today, and finally the visitors of tomorrow who will discover its beauty.
You are commended for the strong love and loyalty you have shown for Colorado and the strength that is necessary to continue making it the best place in the world to live. Be well and play hard, for Colorado is our home.

To T.J. thank you for your support. You are the best.

INTRODUCTION

Throughout the revision of this book, I have pondered the question, "What is Colorado?" There are so many ways to define this state, from its people to its corporate and government base, to its alluring yet formidable Rocky Mountain Range. What I've found, as I've roamed the state, writing and revising *Tours For Free Colorado*, second edition, is that Colorado is the best of all worlds. And that's what I've tried to convey through the selection of tours that you'll find in this guidebook.

The second edition of *Tours For Free Colorado* is bigger and better than ever. It incorporates and brings to life many of your suggestions, with more places around the state and a broader variety of tours. Tours offered by companies, institutions and individuals highlight interesting and intriguing opportunities found nowhere else. The new hidden treasures of Colorado in this guidebook are all free, just like before. All you need to do is get out there, check it out, and answer for yourself: "What is Colorado?"

Enjoy your tours for free!

Jodi Jill

NOTE FROM THE PUBLISHER

Welcome to the *Tours For Free* series. This original idea came from Jodi Jill's love of Colorado and the tours that she found educational, interesting, fun and most importantly, free. BentLight Media, Inc., is pleased to offer this book to Colorado residents, and visitors from other regions so that they may enjoy and explore wonders of Colorado.

All of us here at BentLight Media love tours almost as much as we love making books, so if you have any comments about our book or suggestions for additional tours, we want to hear from you.

John Kellow, Publisher

HOW TO USE THIS BOOK

To make it easy to find interesting tours in the area, Tours For Free Colorado is laid out in five different regions. Within each region, cities are listed alphabetically and the tours within these cities are listed alphabetically by name. If you are looking for a specific tour, reference the index in the back of the book.

THE ART OF TOURING

HERE ARE A FEW BASIC TIPS TO MAKE YOUR TOURING EXPERIENCE THE VERY BEST!

- Before attending a tour call the facility to check the schedule, find out any additional directions and clarify any details that will be necessary for the tour to be enjoyable. The information in this book is current as of our publication date, but we can not guarantee that it will not change.
- Wear comfortable clothes and shoes while touring and layer your clothing to adjust for an unexpected temperature change. Some tours have dress codes, so check it out before you go.
- Don't bring too many items you will need to carry during the tour. Keep what you bring to a minimum.
- Check with the tour guide to find out if it is permissible to take pictures during the tour. Certain companies will not allow photographs to be taken.
- Most tours will make children feel special and welcome. Call ahead if you are unsure.
- Stroller requirements will vary, so if you have a small child call ahead to find out if there are any space limitations.
- Be on time for a reserved tour! If you are going to be late, call the facility to let them know. They may accommodate your unexpected delay or reschedule the tour.
- If you have any questions, ask the tour guide. Keep in mind that they may not have every answer, but most will make arrangements to find the answer if possible.
- Stay with your tour group and ask the tour guide before touching anything.
- Every tour guide will provide the best possible setting for a safe and enjoyable tour, but there are hazards. If you understand the risks and stay alert, you will reduce your chances of getting hurt or damaging equipment.
- Be modest when taking samples. If you would like more, you can always ask after the tour is over.
- Ask for more information! Some facilities will provide brochures at the end of the tour.
- When the tour is complete, take a moment to thank your tour guide. If they did an outstanding job, you should consider sending a card to thank them or let their supervisor know how impressed you were.

■ When touring you need to roll with the punches. If you didn't get the chance to see what you wanted, try again. Remember that the tours are part of a larger operation.

■ Many of the facilities listed have gift shops. While you are under no obligation to buy anything, you will have the chance to purchase one-of-a-kind items in these shops.

TAKING SELF-GUIDED TOURS

Some people might prefer to consume knowledge at their own speed, or perhaps they do not like crowds. No problem! There are listings for self-guided tours so you can explore Colorado at your own pace.

A self-guided tour will not give you the added feature of asking experienced individuals to share their knowledge, but you will still learn plenty. Displays, interactive computers, and photographs will be available. It is important to call the facility to confirm a self-guided tour, especially if the location is far from home.

TAKING GUIDED TOURS

Most Colorado tour guides are pleasant people who will try to accommodate your requests. Whether touring alone, with family or as part of a class, your request will be handled with the same enthusiasm that guides share during the tour. When you call the facility to schedule a tour, it is a good idea to have the following information ready to share:

1. Age range and number of people attending
2. Amount of time that is needed to tour
3. Any special requirements or concerns (e.g. wheelchairs, strollers, people who have difficulty walking long distances, people who are allergic to certain chemicals)
4. Two or three dates and times when the group could conveniently tour

If you are unable to attend the scheduled tour call the facility and let the tour guide know. They will appreciate the call and you will be able to reschedule for a later date. It is also important to let the facility know if the number of people in your group changes, as many tours have guidelines regarding minimum and maximum numbers of people in each group. Keep in mind that a facility might need to cancel a tour, so it is advisable to call and confirm on the day of the tour.

THE EDUCATOR AND COLORADO TOURS

Taking children on tours, whether as school groups, home school families or extra curricular organizations, is a fabulous way to explore and learn! You will give children an experience that will encourage them to ask questions and discover Colorado.

Before calling to schedule a tour, there are a few important details to clarify:

- The number of students attending and their age range

- How the tour will create or enhance the classroom work

- Any special needs or concerns

- Length of time needed for the tour

- Convenient dates for the tour

Once the tour guide knows this information he or she can help decide if their tour would be appropriate for your group. Usually the tour guide will schedule a group tour as a top priority, especially for education. Many of the facilities will provide worksheets and scavenger hunt activity guides that will complement the child's touring experience. Most of the educational tours will offer free items to children, such as book markers, rulers, pencils, and information packets. These little items excite children and encourage them to pay attention to the tour's message. Once you have secured a date, talk with the tour guide to find out what they have to offer. The children will thank you a million times.

TOURING VINEYARDS AND WINERIES

Colorado has many fine vineyards and wineries. From the Front Range to Palisade, these vineyards and wineries produce quality wines for the community. Touring wineries is both entertaining and educational. From the flowery terminology to the fermentation process, visitors leave with a new understanding of one of the oldest beverages known to man. When you are deciding where to tour, an important aspect to consider is the difference between vineyards, wineries and cellars. A vineyard is where the grapes are grown and wine is made. The vineyard might be in its first or fifth year, but no matter how mature the crop, there will be grapes growing on the property. A winery is called such because the wines are made from grapes that are shipped to the facility from another location. By using the term cellars, a company implies that both a winery and a vineyard are on the property, and the harvest used for the wine production is from their vineyard. No matter which tour you decide to take, most of the wineries listed in this book use Colorado grapes.

Another important term to remember is "vintner". He or she is the central figure in the winery, the wine maker. The number of vintners depends on the type of wine they highlight and the number of gallons produced annually.

Depending on the time of the year and how many visitors are in your group, wineries and vineyards welcome guests to view their premises and enjoy their tasting rooms. It is advisable to call ahead to set an appointment. This will allow you to confirm business hours or perhaps arrange a private tour and tasting. The actual time for the winemaking tour will only be ten or fifteen minutes. It will include some history of the business and a basic tour to look at the equipment and facilities. You will enjoy absorbing information about the winemaking process from the vintner. Ask plenty of questions on the tour and you will become a wine aficionado before you leave. The time allotted for the tour will be somewhat limited, but there should be plenty of time for tasting the wines and enjoying the views. Tasting rooms vary as each vintner puts together a room that complements his or her wine. A large selection of wine will be on display in the tasting rooms, and you will be welcome to try a free sample. Some of the tasting rooms feature elegant food items that are for sale, while others highlight wine-related products such as corkscrews. Logo merchandise is available at many of the wineries, and you will always find cases upon cases of wine available for purchase. Most of the tasting rooms have outdoor seating, so you can pull up a chair and relax while you sample the wine. If you decide to bring a picnic, you could buy a bottle of your favorite wine to accompany the meal.

THE COLORADO BREWING EXPERIENCE

There are two major brewing companies and over 50 microbreweries located in Colorado. With such a large selection, how can you tour the breweries and find what you are looking for? Tours for Free has done some of the work for you. Obviously, we can't list all tours in the state, but we have selected ones that offer something unique about the tour or facility, that sets it apart from other breweries. Included are breweries in each region, making it highly likely that you are not far from a great brewing experience!

The major brew tours are standard but easily accessible, and they will give you an overview on how the brewing process works on a large scale. The microbreweries and brewpubs are more down to earth and the choice might be a matter of a taste or location. Each microbrewery is similar in its handcrafted brewing techniques, but the ambiance of the brewery and the style of the beer vary. Becoming a beer connoisseur in Colorado will be easy once you know where to go. The listings of breweries are divided into two categories: brewpubs with restaurants and microbreweries.

In a brewpub the equipment is usually located near the bar and often you will be able to see it when you are seated in the restaurant. A microbrewery usually produces large volumes of beer and will be less likely to sell food.

If you would like to learn how beer is made, a microbrewery or brewpub is the best place to start. The brewer or general manager will be the guide for most of the tours, and the best time to schedule a brewery tour is first thing in the morning or in the afternoon. The normal hours for brewing are 7am – 3pm. The requirements for touring will vary at every location, so call in advance to get specific information. If you decide that a group tour would be perfect, take into consideration the number of people, as many breweries will only allow ten people in a tour group.

During the various brewery tours you will see many different types of grains that are used to make beer. If you are able to look at the grain bags, you will lean what kind of malt is being used and where it originated. The grain is usually cracked and transported to the mash tun where it is mixed with hot water, which causes the starch to covert into sugar. The sweet liquid known as "wort" is drawn off the bottom of the mash tun and pumped to the brewkettle. Once the kettle is full, the wort is brought to a boil and bittering hops are added. Regular hops are added toward the end of the boil to give it a distinct aroma and flavor. The boiling process usually takes about an hour, after which the mixture is allowed to settle. The wort is pumped through a heat exchanger that cools the sweet mixture before it is placed in the fermentation tank. Yeast is added to convert the sugars to alcohol and carbon dioxide. Cold conditioning takes place in the same tank or one nearby. The temperature of the tank is kept at near freezing from two weeks to two months depending on the style of beer. After this process, most beers are filtered, carbonated and bottled. All the breweries have different methods of brewing depending on their equipment and the secret brewing techniques. After the tour you will be invited to enjoy a complementary sample. Brewmasters enjoy seeing how their customers respond to their brews. At many locations you can purchase their products to enjoy at home.

LEVEL OF DIFFICULTY

Tours For Free uses an easy-to-understand rating system for the level of difficulty for each tour. These ratings are helpful to ensure that you have the best possible time on the tour. If you are concerned about a specific tour, you can always call ahead.

EASY: On these tours you can expect a short walk without any climbing of stairs.

MODERATE: On these tours you can expect a longer walk with some climbing of stairs or hills.

DIFFICULT: On these tours you can expect to walk a significant distance, with stairs or hills to climb.

COLORADO

ARVADA

BOULDER

DENVER

GOLDEN

MORRISON

WESMINISTER

DENVER METRO

ARVADA CENTER SCULPTURE GARDEN

The thought of wandering through this garden on a warm summer evening is not a bad one, especially if you are going to be visiting the Arvada Center for the Arts and Humanities, next door. This tour offers an artistic twist that you'll not want to miss. Beginning with the famous "sea-saurus" named Squiggles (see the Squiggles tour), a purple monster sculpture just north of the doors, this tour includes silly and serious exhibits. One of the most interesting pieces here is Dirt Wall, by Vito Acconici. The wall begins outside of the center and works its way in, expanding to over 300 feet. It's made of layers of red volcano rock, Cherry Creek sand, concrete sand, dry sand, red dolomite and top soils applied to 304 panels of varying shapes and sizes, using more than 50 gallons of glue. The artist's message is that earth is the foundation to everything.

You'll also see several pieces by John Young, including *FlatIrons* and *Jack's Piece*, displayed on each of the driveways at the entrance. *Jack's Piece* involves carefully placed native flagstone slabs pointing up to the sky. *The Ramp Piece*, situated inside the parking lot, represents the relationship between elements, and how we apply them in the everyday.

Finally, John Van Alstine's sculpture *Arch #5*, a piece the kids will enjoy, is a minimalist exhibit that uses properties of tension, balance and gravity to make it look like this thing might fall at any minute. This sculpture really stands out – and stands up! Each element is strategically placed to give the illusion that it's off-balance, but *Arch #5* isn't going anywhere!

You'll find the self-guided brochure to the gardens just inside the doors of the facility. It's a great reference for learning more about the artists and their pieces. Wile inside, don't forget to check out the free gallery and mini-museum.

TAKE THE TOUR

WHERE TO GO
6901 Wadsworth Blvd.
Arvada, CO 80003-9985
WHEN TO GO
Self-Guided Tour
Daily
Dawn – Dusk
DEGREE OF DIFFICULTY
Moderate
CONTACT
720.898.7200
www.arvadacenter.org

OLD TOWNE WINERY

TAKE THE TOUR

WHERE TO GO
5659 Old Wadsworth
Arvada, CO 80002

WHEN TO GO
Guided Tour
Tasting Room Hours:
Saturday & Sunday
Noon – 3pm
Reservations Required

DEGREE OF DIFFICULTY
Easy

CONTACT
800.990.WINE
or 303.901.2648

Believe it or not, there are several Front Range wineries that make top-quality wines, and Old Towne Winery is one of them. The grapes used for the vino come from the Western Slope, only a couple of hours away. Christy Angell, the vintner, lives nearby and has been making wines for many years. The perfect combination of her talents and Colorado's grapes makes for some fine blends.

When you stop by the delightful tasting room, you will see the colorful wines waiting to be sampled. There is a display of your choices lined up on the counter, and wine accessories are also available.

Established in 1997, the Old Towne Winery is located in downtown Arvada, near the famous Arvada Flour Mill. The entrance is in the alley. The wines are handcrafted in limited quantities and are total grape varieties. Perfect for a gift from a Colorado company, or you can pick up a bottle to accompany a nice dinner.

SQUIGGLES

TAKE THE TOUR

WHERE TO GO
6901 Wadsworth Boulevard
Arvada, CO 80003

WHEN TO GO
Self-Guided Tour
Daily
Dawn – Dusk

DEGREE OF DIFFICULTY
Easy

CONTACT
720.898.7200

**www.arvadacenter.org
/playground.php**

If you are wondering were to find the "sea-saurus" in the metro area, you'll need to check the Arvada Center Playground. This purplish 343-foot-long animal sculpture has plenty of bends, folds and curves for kids to tour and explore. The friendly monster's name is Squiggles.

Just outside the Arvada Center, on Wadsworth, Squiggles lives comfortably. This is a neat place to take the kids and explore for hours. The main body of Squiggles is a concrete base, sculpted to look like fish scales. Every scale is different in shape and size, and each has a unique hieroglyphic carved into it. You could spend an hour looking at and playing on the monster, and still only see a small section of the scales on the tail. So of course you should expect the kids will want to visit more than once.

From the giant tail that wraps around the playground, to the teeth in the mouth, the kids can touch Squiggles as much as their hearts desire. Thick rubber padding surrounds the giant sea creature, adding a bounce to your step, but also making for a safe play surface.

On August 23, 1998, Squiggles was born, after five years of efforts. Designers engineered it with all kids in mind, but it's especially great for children with disabilities. On this playground kids in wheelchairs can roll up and be part of the action! And kids with visual impairments will benefit from the hands-on quality of Squiggles: Each scale is etched with different pictures and kids can feel their way around! A book about this funny little monster is currently in production for kids to take home.

Before you leave, make sure the family checks out the talking trashcans, only a few steps from Squiggles. The voice you hear is Jim Green's, the same guy you hear on the trains at DIA, and from the noisy grates off of the 16th Street Mall in downtown Denver. The cans project more than 20 different sounds!

During the summer Squiggles gets rowdy and blows off a little steam -- controlled of course. Puffing water through the mouth and off the scales, Squiggles cools kids down on a hot day.

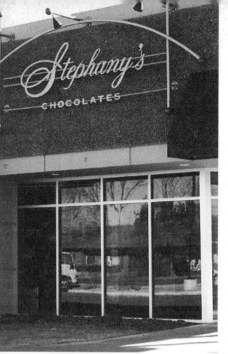

STEPHANY'S CHOCOLATES

Although Stephany's doesn't make chocolates, it prepares wonderful chocolate products. They also produce an almond toffee, which has won "Outstanding Confection" at an international food show held in New York.

The amazing process begins by melting large bars of chocolate into liquid, which is poured into molds. After the molded chocolate has been cooled, an employee adds the finishing touches by painting the eyes, smiles and other small details on the specialty chocolates. Finally, the chocolate is packaged and placed in gift boxes. Stephany's mints are the most popular, as they are well known across the county. Creating the mints is an elaborate process, which requires pouring two layers of chocolate and one layer of a green mint mixture. The candy is layered on top of an old bowling alley table that reaches halfway across the room. After the cooling process is complete, the mints are cut into one-inch pieces and uniquely packaged.

The tour then proceeds to the shipping department, where you'll have a chance to sample the chocolate. In this area you will be shown the various chocolate boxes, which hold the different collections, and you will learn about the mail order process. Stephany's also distributes its chocolates through the seven Colorado stores, and nationwide through specialty shops and the internet.

The tour guide will also show you the double chocolate room, where you will have a serious chocolate experience! The scent of warm chocolate is extremely strong in this room, so be prepared!

You may also have the opportunity to observe the process of creating almond toffee. Every batch of toffee requires 60 pounds of ingredients, which are mixed together in a huge copper bowl. After the mixture has been heated to the appropriate temperature, two people transport the bowl to a large square water-cooling table. The toffee mixture is poured on the table and flattened, while cold water flows across the tabletop. The cooling process continues for about five minutes and the toffee is cut and packaged. An average of 15 toffee batches are produced daily, and it has a shelf life of four to six months.

The tour concludes in the gift shop, which is filled with delightful goodies that you can take home to the family.

TAKE THE TOUR

WHERE TO GO
6770 W. 52nd Avenue.
Arvada, CO 80002

WHEN TO GO
Guided Tour
Monday – Thursday
9:30, 10:30, 11:30am and 1pm
25 People Max per Tour
Reservations Required
Ages: 5+

DEGREE OF DIFFICULTY
Moderate

CONTACT
303.421.7229, ext. 111
800.888.1522
www.stephanys-chocolates.com

AUGUSTINA'S WINERY

Augustina's Winery produces wine that Coloradoans will be proud to drink. Located in Boulder, the winery is nestled up near the foothills of the Rocky Mountains. While it may seem odd that a winery is on the Front Range instead of the Western Slope, it's important to realize that grapes can be easily moved across the Continental Divide. Since the vineyards are only a short distance from the winery, the grapes maintain a superior quality.

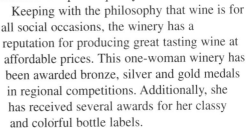

TAKE THE TOUR

WHERE TO GO
4715 N. Broadway B-3
Boulder, CO 80304

WHEN TO GO
Reservations Required
Call for Tasting Room Hours

DEGREE OF DIFFICULTY
Easy

CONTACT
303.545.2047

Keeping with the philosophy that wine is for all social occasions, the winery has a reputation for producing great tasting wine at affordable prices. This one-woman winery has been awarded bronze, silver and gold medals in regional competitions. Additionally, she has received several awards for her classy and colorful bottle labels.

The winery produces Colorado-grown varietal, hybrid and fruit wine blends. The bottles of wine can be purchased in the tasting room or at farmers' markets. You may see the product sold by the glass at gallery showings, theater performances and festivals.

BOULDER COUNTY RECYCLING CENTER

Newspapers, soda cans, and even cardboard can be recycled and reused, and the Boulder County Recycling Center tour explains how recycling works in the Boulder area. Caution though: This is an extremely smelly tour not recommended for people with weak stomachs.

As you pull into the lot you'll see full-size recycling bins, where items to be recycled are placed into openings on the top. There are places for cardboard, aluminum, plastic, paper, paperboard, and glass. Once the bins are full, they are taken back to the recycling center.

The tour starts on the first floor foyer of the center. Recycling information, available at the kiosks, explains what is recycled in the facility. The information is geared mostly toward kids, with the idea of recycling waste into wanted products being the main theme. A nice exhibit of bottles, cans and paper does a good job of conveying what can be recycled and how each person can do his or her part.

The next section of the tour takes you up the stairs and through the door. As soon as you open the door you'll start to smell what awaits you. On the second floor are more exhibits of products made with reusable materials. This is especially interesting, as you may not have known that materials such as plastics

TAKE THE TOUR

WHERE TO GO
1901 63rd Street
Boulder, CO 80301

WHEN TO GO
Self-Guided Tour
Monday – Friday
9am – 5pm

DEGREE OF DIFFICULTY
Moderate

CONTACT
303.444.6634

can be recycled and used for other things such as making a porch in your home.

At the far end of the hallway are cages filled with recyclables, waiting to go through the machines. The machines separate the stuff into appropriate piles, and pick out unwanted materials. From there, the piles are bundled and placed outside in stacks. Usually recycling material is bought by the ton, so each bundle is about the same weight. Look out of the last window to see the bundles.

Trucks full of recyclables drop off more, as the machines run at full speed sorting and piling. It's a never-ending process.

Pick up the recycling brochures available on your way out. They provide a good education on the rules of recycling, including ways to recycle more efficiently and how to interpret recycling symbols.

BOULDER DUSHANBE TEAHOUSE

TAKE THE TOUR

WHERE TO GO
1770 13th Street
Boulder CO 80302

WHEN TO GO
Self-Guided Tour
Daily 10am – 8pm

DEGREE OF DIFFICULTY
Easy

CONTACT
303.442.4993
www.boulderteahouse.com

In 1987, the mayor of Dushanbe, Tajikistan, a small country in Central Asia, announced the decision to send a traditional teahouse to Boulder, its sister city. The elaborate and unique gift was meant to offer the people of Boulder an experience reminiscent of the community gathering places of Dushanbe. The intricate building was originally crafted in Tajikistan by over 40 artisans, and then shipped to Boulder in crates. Four of the original artists came to Boulder to help build the Teahouse in its permanent home.

Dushanbe, the capital of the former Soviet Republic of Tajikistan and home to about 524,000 people, has been Boulder's sister city since 1983. It's location, nestled between Afghanistan, Pakistan and China, in the heart of the Pamir Mountains, is especially relevant to us today.

From the outside, notice the eight ceramic mosaic panels, each displaying patterns of a "Tree of Life." The outside corners of the teahouse are also tiled, carefully placed to reflect beauty for miles away.

When you walk inside the teahouse, look up to the ceiling, which was originally built, carved and painted in Tajikistan. Artists hand carved and painted it with traditional patterns of Persian Art. There are 12 beautifully carved cedar columns, no two alike. The walls of the teahouse are made of plaster panels, expressing the traditional Persian art called "Ganch". Each panel is composed of a number of tiles that come together as a whole. The central area of the teahouse is the copper Fountain of Seven Beauties, named for characters in the fourth poem of Nizami Ganjavi's "Khamsa".

The teahouse is open daily for touring, or for a cup of tea. Traditional seating in several booths is available, as are tables. The smells from the teas are delightful and soothing, and the atmosphere is different from that found in any other teahouse in Colorado – and it's definitely the only one from Tajikistan!

CELESTIAL SEASONINGS

Finding a cup of herbal tea is not difficult in Boulder, and Celestial Seasonings, tucked close to the foothills and Flatirons, is a well-known source for producing the perfect cup.

The factory tour is what you might expect, only better. Starting with their best foot forward, Celestial Seasonings offers complimentary tea -- hot and cold -- in the tasting room. While sipping tea, visitors can view the small gallery that exhibits original art from the product boxes. There is also an unusual display of teapots and cups created by artists all over America.

Once the tour begins, guests go through the corporate office on the way to the production plant. Before entering the plant, a surprise awaits... all guests are required to wear the sanitary hairnets.

After placing a net over the noggin, the tour moves into the huge storage space that holds the ingredients for the teas. The tour guide will reveal the many countries that are used as sources for the plants, and explain the milling process where herbs are prepared for blending.

Next, the tour enters the aromatic green and mint tearooms, which are separate from the rest of the ingredients due to flavor contamination issues. Both rooms are amazing! As you enter, the smells will charge your senses and cause your eyes and nose to tingle.

After cleansing the pallet, the tour proceeds toward the warehouse where the colorful trademarked boxes of Celestial Seasonings are kept. The massive stacks of boxes will hold tea bags for more than 1.3 billion cups that this company produces annually.

The tour guide will direct you around a corner to the machines that bag the tea. You will have the opportunity to see how the bags, made two at a time, are put together on the assembly line. The Celestial Seasonings special flavor packaging assures that nothing will cause the tea to taste different before you buy it at the store.

The tour ends in the gift shop, where tea connoisseur delights are for sale, as well as a large selection of Celestial Seasonings teas. If you're still excited about trying more tea, guests are welcome to return to the tasting room for more samples. Additionally, the Celestial Cafe is right around the corner from the gift shop. Employees and workers from the nearby office complex hang out in this colorful and reasonably priced cafe.

Nineteen-year-old Mo Siegel thought up the idea of Celestial Seasonings while in Aspen. He started by gathering wild herbs in the Rocky Mountains for healthful teas. In 1970, Mo Siegel and John Hay produced the first Celestial Seasonings product in Boulder. The first blend, Mo's 36 Herb Tea, was made with 500 pounds of ingredients and it was packaged in hand sewn muslin bags. Their product was sold to the local health food stores. One of the first herbal teas was Red Zinger, introduced in 1972. Today it is just as popular and continues to provide an interesting flavor with the main ingredient being hibiscus flowers.

Moe Siegel retired in September 2002, to spend more time with his family and to pursue other interests. He's still involved with special projects at Celestial Seasonings.

LEANIN' TREE MUSEUM OF WESTERN ART

TAKE THE TOUR

WHERE TO GO
6055 Longbow Drive
Boulder, CO 80301

WHEN TO GO
Self-Guided Tour
Monday – Friday
8am – 4:30pm
Saturday and Sunday
10am – 4pm
Guided Tour
Tuesday – Thursday only
8am – 4:30pm
Reservations Required
50 People Max per Tour

DEGREE OF DIFFICULTY
Easy

CONTACT
303.530.1442, ext. 299
www.leanintreemuseum.com

Founded in 1974, the Leanin' Tree Museum has one of the largest privately owned collections of Western art in the nation. Their exhibits include over 300 paintings and 85 bronzes. A tour of the museum will give you a full scope of how the company was built and the commitment they have to the promotion of Western Art.

The paintings and sculptures in the museum's collection include artistic interpretations of Native Americans, cowboys, pioneers, frontiersmen, trappers and wildlife. The renderings of the scenery and surroundings represent areas all over the West, before and after residents homesteaded them.

The tour begins downstairs next to the gift shop, and there are large pictures on the wall nearby. The guide will take you through the galleries and you'll notice that there are stories that accompany each picture. From these writings you will get a chance to learn interesting facts that overview how people lived, worked and struggled in the West.

The company occupies 10,000 square feet on two floors, and the upstairs gallery provides a lot of fascinating art to view at your leisure. While it might be difficult to keep kids interested in most museum settings, you will not have a problem here. The museum provides interesting games and activities for children, which include a list of items that can be found in the artwork. These types of activities provide children with a basic understanding of Western art history.

LEANIN' TREE PUBLISHERS

Leanin' Tree is the world's largest publisher of western and wildlife greeting cards. The company also produces contemporary and Christian cards, and you will see over 2,000 in the gift shop.

The tour of Leanin' Tree will give you the opportunity to learn how greeting cards are created and you will also come to understand how a small Colorado company has grown into a leader in the greeting card business.

LEANIN' TREE

In 1949, a handshake between Ed Trumble, a sales representative for Western Livestock and Robert Lorenz, an artist at Colorado State University, started a card company known as Lazy R. L. Ranch. The two men decided to paint western art on Christmas cards and sell them through the mail. The first year of their business was so successful that they had to return payments to some of their customers when they sold out of cards. Today, the company, now known as Leanin' Tree, continues the tradition of creating and selling cards.

The first step on the tour is the production floor, where the employees prepare the boxes that will be shipped to the customers. Farther along you will see the cabinets, which hold all of the cards and items that are available in the catalogs. About 250,000

TAKE THE TOUR

WHERE TO GO
6055 Longbow Drive
Boulder, CO 80301

WHEN TO GO
Guided Tour
Tuesday – Thursday
Reservations Required
12 People Max per Tour

DEGREE OF DIFFICULTY
Easy

CONTACT
303.530.1442
www.leanintree.com

Greetings from Colorado

cards are shipped out daily and the order-filling process is very organized. The guide will take you to an area called Distribution Street, where you will see a huge press that prints four colors at once, and produces the final cards.

The tour will proceed upstairs where ideas for card designs are pitched to the company by writers and illustrators who send in their work. If the design fits into the line of Leanin' Tree cards it will be readied for the presses and a release date will be determined. The presses can print up to 85,000 cards an hour, as they are printed with eight to ten designs per sheet.

After the ink is dry, the paper is moved to a cutting machine, which can cut a four- to six-inch pile of sheets at once. Next they are loaded onto a card-scorer machine that makes an indentation in the middle of the card so it will be ready to fold. The guide will also show you the envelope machine, which is noisy, but fascinating to watch.

Leanin' Tree understands the importance of recycling, and as part of their commitment to the environment, they insist that all of their cards, poster prints and envelopes are printed on recycled paper. The recycling center is located on Distribution Street and it is a definite must-see! All of the product seconds or scraps that are not used in the production are baled together, and these materials are recycled again.

MCGUCKIN HARDWARE

TAKE THE TOUR

WHERE TO GO
2525 Arapahoe Ave.
Boulder, CO 80302
WHEN TO GO
Self-Guided Tour
Monday – Friday 8am – 8pm
Saturday 8am – 6pm
Sunday 9am – 5pm
DEGREE OF DIFFICULTY
Easy
CONTACT
303.443.1822
www.mcguckin.com

McGuckin Hardware is known along the Front Range as the "find anything" hardware store, as they stock over 200,000 items. The store is divided into 18 departments, in addition to the Design Center.

Bill McGuckin founded McGuckin Hardware in 1955. With only four departments, he built the success of the hardware store on his belief in personal service, selection of products and first-hand experience. In 1977 construction began on a new building, which was designed especially for the store, and opened in 1978. The store has grown since then, to a 60,000 square-foot sales floor, and a 51,555 square-foot distribution center. A professional design center is located across the parking lot from the main store.

The self-guided tour begins in the middle of the store and winds through each of the 18 departments. Some of the unique highlights of the inventory include Japanese gardening tools, goat's milk soap an electronic fly swatter, plus a wall full of kitchen gadgets.

The tour winds back toward the nuts-and-bolts department of the hardware store, where Bolt Canyon Aisle is located. There are hundreds of little drawers that hold screws, nuts, washers and bolts, which line the aisle from top to bottom. Don't fret if you're not sure what to buy, as employees who are trained specifically in nuts and bolts can give you the run-down of what to use and how to use it! Farther, you will find the important supplies that are necessary to get your repair work done. From door hinges to wood trim, McGuckin Hardware has a selection of five to twenty choices of the same item, available in different styles and brands.

Since the original owner was an avid outdoorsman, the hardware store continues the tradition by stocking a large sporting good's department. If you are an angler, this is the place for you, as they have over 150 fishing flies from which to choose! The tour concludes in the light center, and if you ever need a lamp, special or plain, this is the place to look!

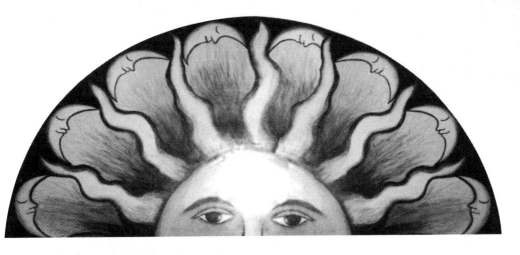

MOUNTAIN SUN PUB & BREWERY

Located on the east side of historic Pearl Street Mall is the Mountain Sun Pub and Brewery, with its sunny logo conveying a feeling of peace and love. The Mountain Sun creates an unusual atmosphere for a brewery. From the tie-dye shirts worn by the patrons to the Grateful Dead music playing in the background, you can easily slip into the '60s, sip a great brew and find yourself lost in the wonders of the Hippie Generation.

The walls are like a brightly painted canvas, which the patrons can enjoy along with the kindness of the Mountain Sun wait staff.

It will be necessary to schedule a guided tour of the brewery that is located in the back of the pub. A tour guide will show you how the brew is made and give you some details about the small area that is known as the beer floor. Don't expect to see the entire operation, as they have the storage for the kegs in a different building.

The brewery has earned awards by local newspapers for best brewery... groovy!

LOCAL'S CHOICE: The Colorado Kind Ale, which has a deep amber body that balances the bitterness, giving it a full-bodied taste.

NATIONAL CENTER FOR ATMOSPHERIC RESEARCH

TAKE THE TOUR

WHERE TO GO
1850 Table Mesa Drive
Boulder, CO 80305
WHEN TO GO
Self-Guided Tour
Monday – Friday
8am – 5pm
Weekends and Holidays
9am – 4pm
Guided Tour
Monday – Sunday at Noon
Reservations Required for
Groups
303.497.1173
DEGREE OF DIFFICULTY
Easy
CONTACT
303.497.1173
www.ucar.edu/ucar/visitor.
html

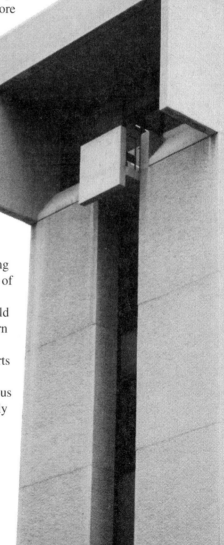

When you drive into the parking lot of the National Center for Atmospheric Research (NCAR), you cannot help noticing the Flatirons and the glorious views from this vantage point. The high mesa where the facility sits is named the Walter Orr Roberts Mesa, in honor of the first director of the facility. On a clear day you will be able to look southeast and see the skyscrapers in downtown Denver; wildlife, such as deer, are a common site on the NCAR property. Making this facility even more spectacular is the building's design, created by famous architect I.M. Pei. Incorporating natural structures, such as the mountains and exposed sandstone rocks into the design, Pei created quite the respite from the city of Boulder, below.

There are two types of tours available at this facility – one with a guide and one without; both are free. Founded in 1960, NCAR's mission is to study the air, sun and weather by collecting data that helps explain the basic elements of the atmospheric system.

Both guided and self-guided tours should begin in the main lobby, where you'll learn a about NCAR scientists and their data. Scientists require information from all parts of the atmosphere to understand the air around the earth. One exhibit shows various research aircraft that NCAR has used to fly around the world collecting samples and doing research. Other exhibits include information about early research equipment. (All of the collected data is stored downstairs in a computer room, which takes up the entire floor. The downstairs area has glass panels, top to bottom, that allow you to see the machines.) My favorite display, though, is the one on microbursts, which are one of the potentially hazardous problems facing airline flights. Microbursts are pockets of enormous energy, the most severe kind called a windshear. NCAR staff has helped pioneer technology to detect microbursts at airports and to help minimize crashes caused by them. The hands-on exhibit allows visitors to create their own microbursts by pumping air into fluid.

Continuing on the upper level, the tour will take you by more than 10 exhibits, each on focusing on a weather element. You will also walk by NCAR's Newkirk White Light Coronal Camera, which is used to obtain data from eclipses of the sun. The library next to the south stairwell is open to the public, and you are welcome to browse and see what the scientists read to keep in touch with current research.

If you decide to tour around lunchtime, the NCAR cafeteria has a great selection of food for a good price, and you will be able to eat outside in the large picnic area.

NATIONAL OCEANIC AND ATMOSPHERIC ADMINISTRATION

TAKE THE TOUR

WHERE TO GO
David Skaggs Research Ctr.
325 Broadway
Boulder, CO 80303
WHEN TO GO
Guided Tour
Tuesday 1pm
Reservations Required
Call 303.494.4091
School Groups
Call 303.497.6286
DEGREE OF DIFFICULTY
Easy
CONTACT
303.497.3333
www.oar.noaa.gov

When you think of weather, you expect to see snow or perhaps the sun shining. If you live in Colorado, you know that both can happen at the same time and it is not even surprising. The tour at the David Skaggs Research Center brings a new perspective on weather and how it changes on a daily basis.

When you pull into the parking lot at the center, take a minute to look at the Flatirons, just west of the building. It is probably one of the best views of the area: The day I was there, the sky was soft blue with small clouds floating by, in no particular hurry. Don't lollygag too much or you will be late for the tour, but do come a few minutes early for the view.

From the parking lot you'll navigate the huge stairway to the building where scientists study the weather and climates of our world. In the lobby, where the tour begins, you'll see hands-on exhibits that will explain some scientific aspects of our world, and the tour guide can help to give even more detail.

More than 900 people work in this NOAA building, which is divided into four sections. There are six labs relating to the atmosphere and climate, along with the regional office of the National Weather Service. The views on both sides of the building and visuals such as posters on the walls, add to the intensity of this hour-long tour, so plan to be stimulated before you leave.

The first stop was the most exciting for me. Here we looked through a glass window, into the Solar Forecast Center. The center has close to 10 different monitors watching the face of the sun by way of digital images from satellites. Staffed around the clock, the center observes solar flares and pattern images useful for future scientific research. Keeping track of the sun prevent damage to

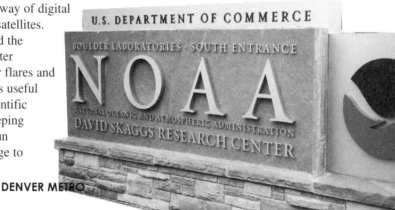

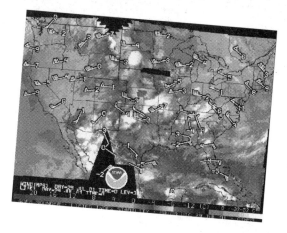

satellites in space won't burn up, and also helps forecast solar flares that may affect earth systems. Items of interest to this scientific field are found in the glass cases on both sides of the room, as well as some interesting and self-explanatory posters. The walls, alone, provide so much information, so keep a sharp eye out for photographs and explanations that are rarely seen outside the building.

Next up was the National Weather Services regional offices, seen through glass windows on the second floor. Computer monitors showed the images that were similar to those we see on the weather segment on television. The overview explains how the weather service uses volunteer weather spotters, radar, satellites, and balloons to keep an eye on atmospheric changes.

The tour stops in front of one exhibit, on the second floor, that is of particular interest. It is a small-scale wind profiler that is part of a new technology developed by the Forecast Systems Laboratory. This new system is a way to monitor moisture and the speed of the winds in the atmosphere, instead of relying on people at the exact area. Currently there are 30 of these new profilers to help study our weather and understand the atmospheric patterns.

After getting the chance to see the central computer facility, you realize just how serious this facility is about weather. Collecting more than a century's-worth of data, these computers keep it readily at the fingertips of scientists and engineers. It is also shared with other weather scientists in the United States and around the world.

The tour ends in the Outreach Room, where you'll see a video covering interesting aspects of the National Oceanic and Atmosphere Administration in the Boulder facility. The tour guide also gives teachers and educators information about different scientific educational projects that can be used at home or in the classroom. The website for NOAA is another great place for young scientists to get more information about what happens at the center.

The information on this tour gives you amazing insight on how our world is evolving and changing everyday. It brings a new appreciation and respect to nature and her bounties.

REDSTONE MEADERY

TAKE THE TOUR

WHERE TO GO
4700 Pearl Street, Unit A-2
Boulder, CO 80301
WHEN TO GO
Guided Tour
Reservations Required
DEGREE OF DIFFICULTY
Easy
CONTACT
720.406.1215
www.redstonemeadery.com

It is known as the drink of the gods, the Vikings, and Shakespeare. What beverage gets such high marks? Mead. It's been a favorite for centuries, and now you can watch it being brewed right in the middle of Colorado.

One of the most famous products is the Nectar, a fast-producing mead made of Colorado clover, wildflower honey and the pulp of blackberries. The product ages for six weeks, the shortest fermentation time of most meads. Redstone Meadery is the only place in the nation that produces draft meads, available at this location and in restaurants around the state. Understand why this is one of the fastest growing meaderies in the country?

This tour covers the basic process of making mead. To make the Nectar, the first step involves adding 360 pounds of Lyons honey to hot water. After a half hour, the brewer adds yeast, yeast nutrient and oxygen, creating pre-mead, which they then place in a temperature-controlled fermenter. After about nine days, the brewer moves the mixture to a cold tank where it conditions. A fruit pulp is added and it sits for another week. When the aging process is complete, the wine is filtered, carbonated and bottled.

On the tour you'll see all the equipment used and get the chance to taste mead, which has different possibilities than grape wines. Mead can be dry or sweet, still or sparkling, and have fruit, herbs or spices added to it. Considering this, you might just find mead to be the perfect drink for your taste.

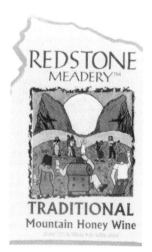

REDSTONE MEADERY™

TRADITIONAL
Mountain Honey Wine

ROCKIES BREWERY

The Rockies Brewery, around for more than 21 years, is proud to be Colorado's first microbrewery. It is their mission to provide beer lovers with superior handcrafted ales, and their reputation has grown along with their sales, which include distribution in 17 states!

The tour of the brewery takes place on two levels. The mash tun and brew kettles are upstairs, and it's great to watch the beer brew while you are sipping away and eating cheese fries. The more technical side of the brewing process takes place downstairs, but this area of the tour requires a guide. One of the most exciting places to check out is the refrigerated area, on the west side of the building. This is where the finished product is kept prior to distribution. The tour also includes an outside portion, where you can view the silos containing malted barley. Toward the end of the tour, you will get a chance to see the bottling setup, which includes a beer-packaging process that was once used at the Coors facility in Golden. If you really want to get into the minds of the brewers and those working in the labs, check out the lab room.

BUFFALO GOLD® PREMIUM ·ALE·

Also available at the brewery is delicious food, and the majority of the items prepared with their beer products. The large patio will give you the opportunity to sit with friends and enjoy the evening, or you might listen to live music featured on certain nights.

LOCAL'S CHOICE: The Singletrack, which is a full-bodied copper ale. It is a light, but tasteful drink to share in the presence of friends.

TAKE THE TOUR	
WHERE TO GO	2880 Wilderness Place Boulder, CO 80301
WHEN TO GO	*Guided Tour* Monday – Saturday 2pm
DEGREE OF DIFFICULTY	Moderate
CONTACT	303.444.8448

UNIVERSITY OF COLORADO AT BOULDER

TAKE THE TOUR

WHERE TO GO
Lower Level
University Club
University of Colorado
Boulder, CO

WHEN TO GO
Guided Tour
Monday – Friday
10:30 – 2:30

DEGREE OF DIFFICULTY
Moderate

CONTACT
303.492.6301
www.colorado.edu

You might be wondering who would want to tour a college campus, except for potential students. The answer: Everyone. In addition to the academic side of this university, there is also its historical significance. The University of Colorado has been in Boulder since 1876, and has seen the community grow as it has grown. Downtown Boulder and CU-Boulder campus share historical relevance as well as physical presence.

The tour at the University of Colorado includes attending classes, experiencing college life, walking the grounds, and viewing the buildings. If you're only interested in learning about its architecture, skip the class session and show up for the walking tour.

The tour begins in the University Club, next to the reception desk. Your student guide will give you a real taste of what college life is like. After the introductions, you'll see some of the more predominate architecture. The original building, constructed in 1876, is the Old Main Building. When you see Old Main, remember that the building wasn't always surrounded by trees, only cacti and grasses. Today, more than 200 of the buildings follow the familiar, rural-Italian style, accented by canopies of trees and flowerbeds.

Depending on the time of day you take the tour, the campus may be full of students. Over 26,000 students are currently attending CU-Boulder, with 1,375

faculty members. The educational opportunities are endless for those currently enrolled, as CU-Boulder offers over 130 undergraduate majors.

The tour weaves through Norlin Library and the music and engineering centers, before it ends up at the center fields, used for soccer and festivals. You'll also see dorms as prospective college kids do, as you'll wander inside and check out campus life.

One of the highlights is walking by Folsom Field. During football season, in the fall, every seat at this facility is filled. While you will get a workout with all the walking, this tour is a chance to learn more about the inner workings of a university.

WHOLE FOODS MARKET

Founded in 1980, Whole Foods Market is the authority on organic and natural foods. Their first store was opened in Austin, Texas, and today they have 136 stores nationwide, including the Boulder store, which opened in 1998. Each store strives to provide fresh fruits, vegetables, meat and other grocery items with a local impression. Whole Foods Market offers a wonderful tour for kids that will give them an overview on how food is grown and what it should taste like.

The tour will begin in the produce department. After the guide discusses how various types of fruit are grown, the kids will learn the difference between organic and conventional produce. One difference is in the color of fruit, and sometimes the answer goes beyond the skin. The guide will explain why organic farmers do not use pesticides or fertilizers, and they will discuss some of the natural methods that help keep the crops healthy and bountiful.

The tour will proceed to seafood department, where you will see an excellent selection of choice fish and seafood; the kids love seeing the big salmon. An overview of the dairy department will follow and you will discover the origins of various milk products, and learn that the eggs sold at Whole Foods Market are from free-range or cage-free hens.

One of the highlights of the tour takes place the bulk section. After taking samples from the various bins, the guide will ask the children to smell different spices, seasonings or grains and try to guess what the item is. The overview of the meat department will include a quick look at the selections in the case, and the guide will discuss how Whole Foods Market meats are different from choices found in a regular grocery store. Whole Foods Market only sells natural meats and poultry from animals that are free of growth hormones and antibiotics.

The guide will lead you through the various aisles in the store, on a path to the bakery department, where the children will learn about the ingredients in various baked goods.

At the end of the tour everyone will receive a goody bag, which is generously filled with items such as fruit leather, stickers and pencils for the children, along with information for the parents. A tour of Whole Foods Market can be geared toward adults as well, and it can be scheduled for groups of 15 people or less, who are interested in learning about the food we eat and how it affects our lives.

The tours at Whole Foods Market vary with the season and age of the group. If you have special interests, it is advisable to call ahead and ask the tour guide if you can be accommodated. Also, don't forget there are other Whole Foods Markets in Colorado, including Cherry Creek and Highlands Ranch, that offer tours.

BOYER'S COFFEE

TAKE THE TOUR

WHERE TO GO
7295 N. Washington Street
Denver, CO 80229

WHEN TO GO
Guided Tours
Reservations Required
Groups of 25 people

DEGREE OF DIFFICULTY
Moderate

CONTACT
303.289.3345
www.boyerscoffee.com

The rich smell of coffee in the morning is what it takes to get up most days. Believe it or not, coffee is a global industry employing millions. Additionally, it is a leading commodity, second only to oil in terms of monies traded worldwide. In Colorado, we have a local coffee company that offers the public an inside glimpse into the small bean responsible for such huge commerce. Started by Bill Boyer in 1965, with only $1,800, the company has expanded rapidly to became a major coffee supplier with premium coffee and tea distributed to more than 2,500 offices, restaurants, and food service businesses.

The tour starts in the coffee house and flagship store at Boyer's Coffee. Some of the more than 125 varieties of Boyer's coffee, along with gifts and teas, are for sale here. Make sure to look above the counters, as the walls are lined with burlap coffee bags from around the world.

In the main building, you'll see how coffee roasting is done. Arabica coffee beans – the world's top-quality beans – begin roasting over an open flame. Although the beans start out green, they turn brown once the heat is on. According to the tour guide, darker coffee means the beans have been roasted with a very hot flame for a longer period of time. Likewise, milder coffees are not roasted as long, at such a hot temperature. Once the beans are roasted to perfection they are cooled with a shot of cold water and rotated in a special machine to release the heat.

There is a roaster, a packaging machine and burlap bags filled with coffee beans. Ground coffee and whole coffee beans are placed into the bags, the air removed and sealed to keep the product fresh. (A fresh pound of unopened coffee can last several months.) On my tour I saw bags marked "Mexico" and "Brazil," indicating the beans' origins. Boyer's has many varieties of coffee, and roasts different ones each day. Look for the bags on the bottom of the machines to know which is the flavor of the day.

The next stop on your tour is the flavoring room. Ever wonder about flavored coffee? Your curiosity will be satisfied here, as your nose go crazy. The overwhelming smell of flavoring oils such as vanilla and Irish cream, compete in this room. Flavored coffees begin as regular beans, and then the flavoring and the beans are tumbled together in special tumbling machines. As the beans circulate, they become specialty beans that take on the taste of the flavoring.

Next stop on the tour is the bean warehouse. Here you will see burlap bags filled with beans and stacked at least two floors high. It is an overwhelming sight! From there, you'll see boxes of coffee waiting to be shipped to loyal Boyer's customers.

The tour concludes back at the coffee shop, where you can grab a "cuppa joe" while thinking about the importance of Boyer's Coffee to the state of Colorado.

THE BROWN PALACE HOTEL

TAKE THE TOUR

WHERE TO GO
321 Seventeenth Street
Denver, CO 80202

WHEN TO GO
Guided Tour
Wednesday and Saturday
2pm

DEGREE OF DIFFICULTY
Moderate

CONTACT
303.297.3111

www.brownpalace.com

The Brown Palace is an icon in the vast history of Colorado's statehood. Mr. Henry Cordes Brown contributed the land that is located only a couple of blocks away from the Colorado State Capitol building. He began planning the Brown Palace Hotel in 1888, and you can view a profile of Mr. Brown etched into the stone near the Broadway entrance.

The Brown Palace was the place to stay when the Colorado Gold Rush hit the state. Opening on August 12, 1892, Mr. Brown knew that he made a good investment as everyone stopped over in Denver when they were traveling into the Rocky Mountain region. He spent 1.6 million dollars for the construction of the hotel, and many travelers or those who found a golden vein in the hills preferred staying at the Brown Palace.

A tour at the Brown Palace Hotel is a step into the history of the hotel and you will learn how the West was developed in the Gold Rush era. There are many interesting things to check out during this tour, as well as afterwards, so plan to stay

a while. You may want to just sit in the atrium and soak up the hotel's beauty, as it is a very moving experience.

Mr. Brown hired the architect, Frank E. Edbrooke, to design the hotel in an Italian Renaissance style. Mr. Edbrooke is also famous for designing other landmarks such as the State Capitol building. He created the exterior of the hotel using Colorado red granite and Arizona sandstone. James Whitehouse, a commissioned artist, created 26 stone medallions and each of them display a native Rocky Mountain animal. These portraits can still be seen between the seventh-floor windows.

The interior design includes the country's first atrium lobby. The flowing lines of the design create a visual beauty as well as an additional security feature. The balconies rise eight floors above the lobby, and they are surrounded by cast railing with ornate panels. Two of these panels were placed upside down, but no one knows if this was intentional. The lobby, Onyx Room and the eighth-floor ballroom are decorated with imported white onyx from Mexico. A total of 12,400 surface feet of onyx was used in the hotel.

Because of the triangular shape of the building, all of the rooms have windows that face the street.

The Brown Palace has kept the original beauty created by Edbrooke, and the management has added several features to accommodate today's traveler. At one time the hotel had 400 rooms available for guests. Today, with the expansion of office space, there are 230 rooms available. On the premises you will find the most delightful restaurants and shops, which offer one-of-a-kind items. The atrium is a wonderful place to enjoy the afternoon with a proper English tea service and the sound of beautiful piano or harp music.

The Brown Palace Hotel has many stories to share about the guests who have stayed on the here. An amusing story involves the Eisenhower suite, where one can see a dent in the fireplace molding, which is said to have been made by a wayward golf ball that Ike hit while practicing in the room.

No matter where in Colorado you live or if you are just passing through, a tour of the Brown Palace Hotel is well worth your time. You will learn more about Colorado and see how The Brown Palace treats travelers like royalty.

COLORADO STATE CAPITOL

Gold was discovered here in 1858, which was three years before Colorado became a U.S. territory.
Knowing that the population would continue to grow, the United States Congress officially granted territory rights on February 28, 1861. The word "Colorado" is derived from the Spanish word meaning "red."

The familiar sight of the gold dome over the capitol is 272 feet above the ground. It was a gift from Colorado miners and the 200 pounds of gold was mined in the mountains to the west.

The guided tour begins at the information desk with an historic overview of Colorado. In the middle of the first floor rotunda there are grand staircases with 77 marble steps and 176 brass balusters. Looking down the stairs you'll see eight striking murals on the first floor walls. Completed in 1940, the murals represent an extraordinary collaboration, between artist Alan True and poet Thomas Hornsby Ferril. You will discover the stories behind these murals and learn about survival in the West.

For those interested in witnessing the political system in action, touring between early January and April may give you the opportunity to see the Senate Chambers and the House of Representative Chambers. The Governor's office, the Lieutenant Governor's office and the State Treasurer are all located on the first floor.

The Colorado state flag, which was adopted in 1911, is flown on the front lawn and inside the capitol. It's interesting to note that each color of the flag has a special meaning for the state. The color blue represents the sky, gold is for the metal found in the soil, red represents the color of the soil and white is for the mountain snow.

During the final leg of the tour you will be able to photograph the special granite

step located on the west side of the building. The step is inscribed with the words: "One Mile Above Sea Level." Well, sometimes you can't believe everything you read and this is one such case. In 1969, students from the engineering school at Colorado State University found it to be inaccurate, and a geodetic survey plug was placed three steps above the inscribed step to accurately account for the one-mile-high mark.

It took more than 22 years to complete the Colorado State Capitol building, and most materials are from the state. The outer walls are granite from Gunnison, the sandstone foundations are from Fort Collins, the marble stairs and floors are from Marble, and the rose onyx is from Beulah.

DENVER CITY AND COUNTY BUILDING

TAKE THE TOUR

WHERE TO GO
1437 Bannock Street
Denver, CO 80202
WHEN TO GO
Wednesday
10 am, Noon, and 2pm
DEGREE OF DIFFICULTY
Moderate
CONTACT
720.913.8464
www.denvergov.org

This building stands out, year-round, but it's especially alluring when the lights are turned on for the Christmas season. Your tour guide will share some of the interesting history and architecture of Denver City and County Building, so it is worth the visit even when it's not the holiday season.

The building took 26 years of planning and was completed in 1932, under the leadership of nearly 40 local architects. Among the outstanding features of this Beaux-Arts Neoclassical-style building is the carillon clock tower, topped with a golden eagle. The building was part of late Mayor Speer's "City Beautiful Movement," and the 450,000-square-foot structure is just as impressive inside as it is outside. Inside, varieties of marble are used, and Colorado-themed murals and oad adorn the rooms.

Large bronze doors open into a lobby featuring panels of Colorado travertine, a native limestone formed by deposits from the mineral springs. Imagine that there are eight 19-foot-tall Colorado travertine columns in the rotunda! If you didn't know better, you would probably have thought the stone was marble. In the foyer of the main entrance, notice the extravagant use of rock on the floors and walls.

The Council Chamber is another interesting place. Denver's City Council members meet in room 451 every Monday to discuss the concerns of the Denver community. Of course, the meetings are probably pretty official, but the room seems quite comfortable. There's an assigned place for each of the 13 decision-makers, as well as seating in the old-fashioned pews for the general public.

As time moves on, the occupants of the building will change. It is expected the Mayor's Office and the Denver City Council will continue to work here, even as some of the crowded city offices move across the street.

DENVER NEWSPAPER AGENCY

This tour of the Denver Newspaper Agency covers the process of printing the news from the conception of the idea to the actual writing, editing, and laying out of the story. The tour begins in the composition room and ends with the finished newspaper.

The production department of the Denver Newspaper Agency creates the most technologically advanced newspaper in the western region. This state-of-the-art equipment was developed overseas and installed in the Denver facility. While you will see the main components of the pressroom, this tour will also show how the Denver Newspaper Agency has effectively brought technology to Colorado.

The tour starts in the long hallway just past the foyer. The tour guide, usually a retired Denver Newspaper Agency employee, will lead the way and describe how the operation works. Having this type of tour guide is a great opportunity. It provides some interesting insight on how the newspaper works on a personal level. On the tour, you may hear some loud noises so the guide thoughtfully provides earplugs for those with sensitive ears.

After getting information about the organization, the tour will head to the bottom of the presses. Mechanical robots move around the area, carrying huge rolls of newspaper to the needful presses. Each robot moves swiftly to the press; there the newsprint is moved off the robot's arm and placed onto press rollers to be readied for the printing. Past the robots you will get the opportunity to see the paper room.

In the warehouse, you will see newsprint on huge rolls, filling the room. There was a forklift operator moving those big wheels of paper to the robots when I was there, so watch out when you go.

The next part of the tour deals with the plates used for the presses. Each page of the newspaper must have a plate. The information from the composition room comes into the production plant and a negative of the page is made. After the negative is checked for perfection, the negative is placed on an aluminum plate. A strong bolt of light is cast upon it, similar to the intensity of standing directly in the sunlight, and the plate is removed and put in developer. The chemical is squeezed off and a gum is put on the plate to keep the image ready for the presses. A hole is punched into the plate so it will catch on the press rollers. The process is repeated for each part of the paper.

While in this area, you will likely hear the next part of the tour, the pressroom. To me this is the most sensational part. You are taken into the room where the presses are working. The noise sounds like a million happy lions are roaring at the same time, and the quick movements of the machine make your eyes cross. The presses stand three stories high on both ends of the room.

The paper comes through the bottom of the press, then up through the rollers. First, the ink is put on the plates. As the image comes off the plate, it is reversed to the roller. The paper is smashed between the first roller and a second roller, which receives the image. This process is known as offset printing. The printed paper continues down the line, is creased, folded, cut, and each piece is caught on a clasp. The paper is then electronically moved to a conveyor belt across the top into a second room. As the paper continues, it is pulled down into a large wheel that collects it. A wheel can hold hundreds of newspapers until the day of publication. Newspaper wheels are all around the area, which hold sections like travel, books, or business. The wheels are then moved to another part of the room and stored. When the corresponding day of the wheel section arrives, the wheel is unwound and the sections are put together. The crease easily opens for the remaining sections to be placed inside. Also in the second room, you will see employees collate all the different advertisements of the newspaper for a particular day, such as the Sunday edition. Machines, using air power, pick up the sections and put them in the appropriate spots making the paper ready for the reader.

The Denver Newspaper Agency is very conscious of the environment so you will get to look at the recycling center of the facility. There are large containers for used paper, ink, and other recyclable products. Before leaving this area, check out the scale built into the floor. If you take a small group, you can see what you weigh collectively. At the end of the tour you will walk into the hallway where you came in, but before you go ask your guide to tell you the story behind the palm tree.

DENVER NEWSPAPER AGENCY

Every morning on the front porch we can find our newspapers. On the cover page, the important happenings of Colorado and the world are splashed in ink. Inside the paper we can search for upcoming events, stories about people in our community and information needed to be part of society. But do you know how the paper is actually put together, and have you considered all the dedicated people who work endless hours to make the newspaper possible? The tour at the Denver Newspaper Agency is a great eye-opener for anyone who takes Colorado's news for granted.

Now I know what you are wondering: Who is this Denver Newspaper Agency? For those of you who remember manually changing the television dial, you'll have another change to get used to: The Denver Post and the Rocky Mountain News worked out an agreement and formed a company to manage the day-to-day business:

TAKE THE TOUR

WHERE TO GO
400 W. Colfax Avenue
Denver, CO 80204
WHEN TO GO
Guided Tour
Reservations Required for
Large Groups
ages: 10+
DEGREE OF DIFFICULTY
Easy
CONTACT
303.892.5002
www.denvernewspaper
agency.com

the Denver Newspaper Agency. The best part is both have separate newsrooms. Technically, the only difference since the merger is that there are no longer two weekend papers. The tour was not affected by this change either; in fact, it brings out the best of Colorado's journalism.

Since the Denver Newspaper Agency has two tours, this highlighted tour focuses on how an idea evolves into a story and how the story is taken to the presses. The second tour starts with the presses and wraps up with information about how the newspapers get to your front porch. I encourage you to check out both tours to get the full spectrum of the newspaper business.

In the foyer, the group begins to see the value of the huge building. My tour had kids as well as adults, so our guide covered a spectrum of information. All the guides are retired employees of the Denver Newspaper Agency, a unique quality for a tour. They do share personal stories with the group – a special treat for those of us who hunger for more information on how the business works.

The Denver Newspaper Agency has a large building on West Colfax that houses the Rocky Mountain Newspaper Editorial, but on the tour you will only see the main areas. The tour starts next to the giant monster machine in the north front window. In 1928, the Mergenthaler Linotype model 25 was moved to Colorado.

This simple machine was once used to produce the first editions of newspapers in Colorado. Work was done by hand to make a quality newspaper and compared to the machines today it is so amazing.

The tour then leads upstairs, where the journey into the minds of reporters begins. The first room you are led to is the editorial boardroom. In this big office space, editors gather around this large table and discuss the possible news stories for the next day. On the walls you view the front pages of papers in weeks past. According to our guide, the newspapers are stuck on the walls to remind the editors the quality of work demanded for the newspaper in future issues.

The tour then heads directly for chaos, better known as the newsroom. In this area you will see people madly typing on their computers or talking on the telephone to complete their news stories. The idea for any news story comes from a source (like the police scanner or a tip on the phone), and then checked for details and facts. From there, a reporter talks to an editor about writing a story you might see in the newspaper. Once approved, the writer will start writing, but not before checking all the facts again and finding out more information. The reporters in this area really need to concentrate on their stories, but a few will take the time to answer questions, especially if you run across reporter Rebecca Jones. She took time for our group to chat and answer questions we had about the process.

The tour then moves through the sports department and if you are lucky you might get to meet artist Drew Litton, a regular contributor to the sports pages. He gave us some interesting insight on what is expected of his job and the responsibilities he has as an artist.

After a story has been written, edited and rewritten it is ready to be laid up in the paper and placed with the necessary photographs to accompany the story. All of this process is done in the composing department. Relying heavily on computers, the workers make the combination of words, art and pictures eye-pleasing. Once the layout is finished the sheet is then digitally wired over to the Denver Newspaper Agency Washington Street Facility, where it completes the final process before being put to bed on the presses.

One department you do not see on the tour, but is important to know about, is the advertising department. This department is divided into two sections, classified and display advertising. Advertisers are important to newspapers, as they are how the newspapers make money to survive.

The first half of the tour leaves you with a new respect on how the newspaper is put together. It is surprising the people in the newspaper business are not crazy, as they work with so much stress to meet deadlines and need to get all the facts straight everyday.

DENVER PUBLIC LIBRARY

The Denver Public Library offers a tour that will give you an opportunity to learn about the architecture, as well as everything that is special on the inside!

The tour begins on the first floor, and the guide will share a few basic facts that will familiarize you with the library. These facts are interesting and amazing! For example, if all of the shelves in the central library were lined up along I-25 you would have bookshelves from downtown Denver to the Loveland exit.

Take a look at the limestone floor on the first level and you will see fossils embedded in it. The limestone is from quarries near Eichstatt, Germany, which have been in operation since the Romans occupied the area about 2,000 years ago. The two most common fossils are the coiled-shaped ammonite and the bullet-shaped belemnite.

TAKE THE TOUR

WHERE TO GO
10 W. Fourteenth Avenue Parkway
Denver, CO 80204
WHEN TO GO
Self-Guided Tour
Daily
Guided Tour
Monday – Saturday
11am – Noon
Sunday 2pm
DEGREE OF DIFFICULTY
Easy
CONTACT
720.865.1111 or
720.865.1330 (for groups of 10+)
www.denver.lib.co.us

The guide will take you to each level in order to view the different parts of the library, and will explain the daily interactions with the patrons. You will be able to view artworks throughout the tour, so take a moment to make mental notes on where to return after the tour, if you want to revisit the art that you liked.

The most elaborate artworks in the library can be seen in Schlessman Hall, which is on level one, near the main entrances. Look upward and you will be able see the paintings, or you can get a closer look by taking an elevator to level two. The artworks of Edward Rucsha show how the settlement of the West was accomplished. The artwork covers over 70 canvas panels, and you'll definitely get a sense of the struggle that was shared by the frontiersman. The Western History and Genealogy Department is located on the fifth level, and it is a highlight of the tour.

The collection in this department focuses solely on the American West. On the south side there is a picture of Ute Native Americans wearing their peace metals, and I believe this picture is worth the tour alone. The braves in this photograph are lifelike, and one can clearly see that they were courageous individuals.

The Magazine Department, on the third level, has 2,300 current subscriptions of periodicals and 100 newspapers available for the classes to read. The US Printing Office repository is located on level four, where you can view the entire US patent collection from 1790 forward. Other publications located here include the Congressional Notes and rules for the Environmental Protection Agency.

There are usually many people reading or studying throughout the library, but these people do not get to sit at the "special" table. The table, which is from the "Summit of the Eight" world economic conference in 1997, is located in the Library Executive Offices on level seven, and it is used for weekly library meetings and conferences.

The tour will conclude at the Library Store, which is very impressive and comparable to the Library of Congress gift store in Washington D.C.

GOVERNOR'S MANSION

Touring the Colorado Governor's Mansion is a great opportunity to learn more about the past and present governors and their families. You'll hear how the governor entertains important heads of the state, as well as national figures. You might be overwhelmed by the extravagant pieces of art and stone, which are difficult to find anywhere else in the state. The mansion has been extensively renovated and you'll see first-hand how that has brought the house up to date. Additionally, everything is designed with the entire room in mind. Carpets are specially made to match furniture and artwork, coordinating the whole room.

The tour covers five adjoining rooms located on the first floor. The remaining floors are the private residence and the closest you will get to that area is looking up the stairway. Listen carefully to the tour guide and you will hear about more than 20 countries that have shipped decorative art and stone works for display in this building.

The first areas you'll see are the vestibule and entry hall. The next stop on the tour is the drawing room: Look out the windows, but don't forget to look up! The chandelier in this room is one of only three in the United States that was originally in the White House. It is extremely beautiful and it has the sheer elegance of Washington D.C.

The library is one of the most intriguing rooms on the tour: It's right out of a Sherlock Holmes book; friendly yet extravagant, this room has tons of written works, but you won't spend too much time here, as the guide will soon lead you to the Palm Room. The whiteness of this room has much to do with the extensive marble that decorates the area. As far back as 12 terms, the First Ladies of Colorado have been adding new items to this room, including pieces from Italy.

Next you will be taken to the dining area, with its specially designed carpet that matches the furnishings. In this room a special carpet was designed to match the furniture in the room. This is the only room in the house that seems dark so it may take a moment for your eyes to adjust. The tour ends in the family room, formerly used as an office, music room and billiards parlor. It's now furnished with a lovely bar, above which the ceilings are painted and etched with figures that have been there for more than 50 years. The tour ends through the side exist, into the gardens.

TAKE THE TOUR

WHERE TO GO
6th and Logan
Denver, CO 80203

WHEN TO GO
Guided Tours
June – August and early
December

DEGREE OF DIFFICULTY
Easy

CONTACT
Colorado Historical Society
303.866.3682
www.coloradohistory.org

HAMMOND'S CANDY

TAKE THE TOUR

WHERE TO GO
4969 Colorado Boulevard
Denver, CO 80216

WHEN TO GO
Guided Tours every 1/2 hour
Monday – Friday
9am – 2:30pm
Reservations Required for
Large Groups

DEGREE OF DIFFICULTY
Easy

CONTACT
303.333.5588
www.hammondscandies.com

When you pull into Hammond's parking lot, you will know by the peppermint and cinnamon smells floating into your nostrils that you've arrived. Hammond's makes candy by hand and gives a great 25-minute tour to guests who are interested in the old-fashioned process. Watching the candy canes, lollipops and ribbon candy being crafted is worth its weight in candy!

As with any food tour, this one, too, begins with the official "handing-out-of-hairnets" ceremony. The required crazy-looking net is placed evenly on the noggin, then guests move on to watch a simple video about Hammond's and the candy-making production. Once the video is over, your group will walk into the packaging area where employees poised at different stations fill orders. As you might guess, Christmas is the busiest time of the year; what you may not realize is that production for the season begins in late summer. The packaging I saw on the tour was quite simple: Different types of candy were placed into ready-made boxes and bags and were then weighed and counted. There were chocolates, but mostly I saw hard candies such as ribbons, lollipops and straws. The smell in the packaging room is very strong and sweet: Just keep in mind that you can only look, as there's no sampling here.

The next part of the tour highlights the actual candy-making process in kitchens where sweets are made by hand, daily. Whether you get to see candy canes being made or lollipops being hand-twisted, you'll appreciate how much work goes into the job. During my visit, I watched miniature cinnamon pillows--- hard, striped candies no bigger than a fingernail---being made from raw ingredients to finished products, mostly in 50- 60-pound batches. Making pillows is a two-part process: The outside shell, with stripes; and the inside that holds most of the flavor. Once the ingredients are heated to a perfect consistency the batch is poured onto a steel slab to cool. As it cools, the candy is separated into smaller portions so coloring and flavoring can be added.

With red-and-white pillows, the red is simply coloring, but the white is made by a pulling machine, stationed close to the viewing window, which uses air and two straight "arms" to work the candy. Once the coloring process is complete, the red and white are sliced together, looking like the perfect flat candy cane. The next task is to work the flavorful center. A portion of candy that was set aside earlier is put into the pulling machine to be worked for consistency and to achieve the white color.

Once the candy is ready, the candy-maker adds flavor, pulls it some more to evenly distribute the flavor, and removes it from the machine to be rolled for the center piece. The two pieces are put together, making a large log. Then the hard work begins. A candy-maker manually pulls one end of the candy log, until it stretches to the thinness of a pencil. The pulling must be steady and consistent to keep the colors even while the candy is cooling. As the candy begins to set like stone, it gets harder and harder to pull. The end of the candy is then hand-fed through a press that pops small miniature pillow candies out the other end.

One of the nice things about this tour is that it's easy for all guests to see the process. Hammond's built a platform that allows even the smallest of kids to look in the window. Mirrors and signs also help you follow along as the guide talks into a microphone.

Hammond's Candy was founded in 1920 and continues to make old-fashioned candy as it did when the company first began. A few simple rules still apply: Make everything by hand and avoid wasting ingredients by reheating excess and using it in the next batch.

When the tour is over you can choose a treat from a big basket of candy before entering the small gift shop where you can buy sweets and gift baskets, and see--- on the north wall---an example of the five-pound lollipops sold during Christmastime. But what's really special about this tour is that you'll take away more than just sweets: You'll leave understanding that Colorado commerce isn't just dependant on computers and real estate, but on good old-fashioned industry, too.

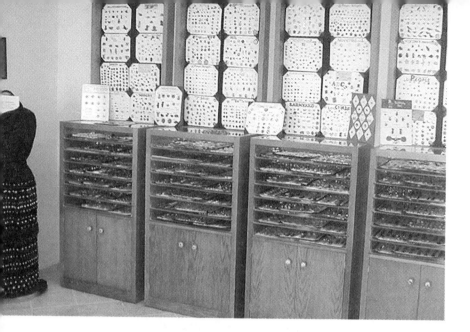

JHB INTERNATIONAL

Have you ever considered the important role buttons play in our lives? I hadn't. But after touring Denver's JHB International, beginning with the Button Museum, I gained a whole new appreciation for buttons, and have even begun my own small collection.

In June, 1969, founder Jean Barr got involved in the international commerce of buttons. Today, her company is known worldwide for simple buttons, novelty buttons, collector thimbles, and more.

The tour begins in the Button Museum, with thousands of buttons displayed on themed cards, along with their series numbers. For example, a card with an ocean theme may include dolphin, whale, and seashell buttons. In the museum are seemingly endless cards of all the buttons distributed worldwide over the past 30 years. But that's not all: As you approach the elevator you'll see an extraordinary collection of thimbles, too, ranging from elegant to everyday.

The main function of JHB, however, is as a wholesaler, buying and selling buttons from everywhere on the globe, including Asia, Africa and Europe. The tour shows you the process step by step. First, single samples come into the facility on cards, and quantities are ordered from them by weight. When the buttons arrive here, they're weighed---not counted---to make sure the order is correct. They're then evaluated for uniformity and quality before being given the "OK". If they're approved, the buttons go into large plastic bags and onto the next step. Rejects are tagged and shelved for return. Judging by the entire wall devoted to this step, it's obvious how important quality control is to JHB.

Next, usually two to four buttons are put onto small cards for retail sale by craft, fabric and other specialty stores. Most buttons are affixed by machines, which is a very labor-intensive process. Each button is placed, manually, under the top of the machine, which then runs a wire through the buttonhole and into the paper to which it attaches. All the while the machine is powered by a person pumping a foot pedal. When I toured, there were at least six machines running, and piles of buttons waiting to be placed on cards, one at a time.

The other method used to affix buttons is by hand. Some novelty buttons, such as ones looking like Santa Claus, are too fragile to run through the machine. These are put onto special cards with two small holes punched in the middle. A person runs wire through the buttonholes, into the holes on the card, then twists it in the back and secures it with tape.

Once on the cards, all buttons are checked again for quality, approved, and then inventoried into immaculately organized boxes that look like card catalogs in a library. When a retailer places an order, a "runner" packages the order and fills the request.

When you think of Colorado, you probably don't think of buttons. But after you take this tour, you'll see how one Colorado woman has made the state the button capitol of the world!

KUSA TV 9NEWS

TAKE THE TOUR

WHERE TO GO
500 Speer Boulevard
Denver, CO 80203
WHEN TO GO
Guided Tour
Reservations Required
DEGREE OF DIFFICULTY
Easy
CONTACT
303.871.9999
www.9news.com

A tour of 9News covers the nuts and bolts of the television industry. It overviews how a newscast is put together, and how the station runs continually 24 hours a day, seven days a week. KUSA-TV, which is part of Gannett Broadcasting, has been a staple in the Denver-metro area since the early days of television, and they employ nearly 200 Coloradoans.

The tour begins in Master Control, where the station receives satellite feeds from around the country. Television shows and commercials are transmitted to this area in order to be reviewed and played during the day. It's amazing how many television screens are in this little room: I believe there are more than 30! There is an electronic board that programs all of the televisions and keeps the station running.

The tour proceeds to the control room of the news studio, which is where the actual news programs are put together. Following a news rundown sheet, the news program is divided into stories and sections. The most important news airs first, followed by weather and sports. The people working in the control room make sure the rundown sheets are followed, and they cue up the graphics as well. They also talk to the newscasters through their earpieces, in order to let them know if there is a late-breaking news story. The control room employees make the newscast look its best.

From the control room the tour will move down a hallway, where you will see the booths that are used to view tapes that might be used for the news. Here you will see more television sets, and while some of them are used to review and edit film for the news, others are transmitting live feed that employees watch to determine if a story will even be covered on the news.

The tour will continue on to the newsroom, which is quite a sight! There are many desks lined up where people work to capture the news. Reporters and on-air personalities are busy writing their news stories or going over possible leads. Each person covers the news on a beat. For example, some of the journalists are assigned to the police beat; others may be responsible for animal stories or news happening on the Western Slope.

The Weather Center is connected to the newsroom. If the weather is good, you will have a chance to see the fish. It's not a real fish, just a rubber one, which is placed on a makeshift fishing pole to symbolize that it is a nice day. The Weather Center utilizes different satellite pictures to help predict the weather. Some of the images are easy to understand, but others are extremely complicated and need to be interpreted by a meteorologist. Using these different satellite images, the weather reporter is able to compile all of the information in order to determine the forecast. The 9News Backyard is where meteorologists do their weather forecast. Here they predict the forecast and provide a realistic setting for the current weather. 9News is the only station in the state that has a backyard and it is a must-see on the tour.

One of the highlights of the tour will be watching a live news broadcast, which will give you the chance to understand everything you learned about the station. The broadcast will allow you to see everything that is not seen on your television at home. The cameras move automatically and the floor director will point to a particular camera that the anchor needs to look at. You will be able to follow along with what the news anchor is saying, as the story is scrolled on the television monitors around the studio. During the commercial breaks the anchors study their news scripts and prepare themselves for the next segment.

This tour will give you the opportunity to come away with some valuable information about broadcasting and you will understand why television stations are an important part of the community.

SANDLOT BREWERY AT COORS FIELD

TAKE THE TOUR

WHERE TO GO
2145 Blake Street
Denver, CO 80205

WHEN TO GO
Guided Tour
Reservations Required

DEGREE OF DIFFICULTY
Easy

CONTACT
303.298.1587

Founded in 1995, the Sandlot Brewery was the first brewery established in a National League Baseball park. Currently owned by Coors, the Sandlot is known for their Blue Moon Ale, which was originally only available at the brewery, but it is now distributed around the nation. There are six varieties under this label, which are produced at the Coors plant in Golden. The tours are usually available around lunchtime or by appointment.

This is the perfect place to gather after a game at Coors Field, but they are open year-round. You will find a high-energy and exciting atmosphere, which complements Colorado and the Rockies.

The process of the brewing is standard, but the names of the ales are quite special. Each one is related to the baseball field and provides some insight into baseball jargon. One of the more interesting names is the Squeezeplay Wheat. It is described as cool and refreshing, much like a late afternoon spent watching a game in the stands. Another, Slugger's Stout, is known to be the heaviest hitter of the Sandlot Beer selection.

LOCAL'S CHOICE: The Right Field Red Ale, which has a "fiery nature that will stay with you, even during extra innings!"

UNITED STATES MINT

A tour of the Denver Mint will give you an overview of how coinage is produced. You will also have an opportunity to learn about the historic value of the building, in which the mint was founded over 96 years ago.

Upon entering the building you will be led to a room with exhibits about the history of the money-making process. A guide will join you, and the tour will officially begin upstairs. There are exhibits along the walls displaying different types of currency that is used around the world today. You will also have the opportunity to see the immense nickel column display, which holds 80,335 nickels, the equivalent of $4,016.75 or 845 pounds. This is a spectacular sight!

The tour will proceed to the second-floor overlook, where the guide will instruct you to look down at machines making pennies, nickels, dimes and quarters. You will be able to watch the process as the press machine stamps both sides of the metal blanks, making them coins. You will also have a chance to learn about the way money was made in the Old West, and you will also see interesting artifacts relating to how the government protected the currency.

You'll then be taken to the bagging area, where loose coins are counted by a machine and placed in bags for transport. There is a wonderful gift shop located in the building, which has a lot of coin-related merchandise for sale. The tour will end outside, along the magnificent walkway in the front of the building.

TAKE THE TOUR
WHERE TO GO
320 W. Colfax Avenue
Denver, CO 80204
WHEN TO GO
Guided Tour
Reservations Required
Monday – Friday
8am – 3pm
DEGREE OF DIFFICULTY
Easy
CONTACT
303.405.4761
www.usmint.gov

UNITED STATES POST OFFICE

GENERAL MAIL FACILITY

A tour of the U.S. Post Office General Mail Facility will give you the opportunity to learn more about various mail procedures. The tour will begin in the lobby of the facility, and the guide will give you an overview about the counter services in the post office and the different ways that mail can be processed. The tour will proceed to the back room, where you might be overwhelmed by what you see, as this facility cancels 1.4 million pieces of mail daily! There are 102 docks in the building, from which mail is continuously loaded or unloaded from an average of 800 vehicles.

The incoming mail is placed in seven-foot wire carts and there are plastic tubs inside them that hold the letter-size mail. The carts are transported to the middle of the room where the sorting equipment is located. The mail containers are loaded onto a conveyer belt and moved through rollers, which make the initial sweep to push out the oversized and overweight letters that might cause the machines to jam. Machines that handle odd sizes sort those letters and envelopes. The regular size envelopes pass through the second sweep, then up a conveyor belt to another machine that places them lengthwise in an orderly fashion. The letters are placed in carrier boxes and employees move them to the next machine, which is computerized. If the computer can read the address and acknowledges the information, it will print a bar code on the front of the envelope. The next machine reads the bar code, which indicates what part of the country the individual pieces will go to. After the mail is placed in the appropriate tub, they are sealed and prepared for delivery.

The mail destined for Denver is loaded on a special machine that sorts it by zip code. After this process is complete, the machine is reprogrammed to sort the mail for the individual carriers, which includes placing it in order of the street addresses within the route.

Overall, the process of sorting mail is elaborate and a tour at the United States Post Office General Mail Facility is fun and full of interesting information.

UNIVERSITY
OF DENVER

The University of Denver is the oldest University in the Rocky Mountain region. Colorado governor John Evans founded the school in 1864, and this tour offers a full hour of interesting facts and historical relevance of one of the top 100 national universities ranked by U.S. News & World Report.

Construction began in 1892 on the University Hall, the first building on campus. At the time money was tight, and in the early 1900s the building was almost bought by a glue company. Chancellor Henry Buchtel was responsible for lobbying hard and saving the building. Your tour will actually start in this building at the Office of Admissions. It's interesting to remember that the building's foundation rests at exactly 5,280 feet above sea level.

From there your tour will weave around the campus, highlighting some of the more significant buildings. The Mary Reed Building, named to honor donor Mary Reed, opened in 1932 as a library; today it houses administration offices. Another building of interest is the Margery Reed Hall. Name after Mrs. Reed's daughter, the 1931 building is the current home of the Theater Department, the little Theatre and the Studio Theatre. Other academic departments also call this home. In the past, the

TAKE THE TOUR

WHERE TO GO
2199 South University
Denver, CO 80208

WHEN TO GO
Guided Tour
Monday – Friday
11am, 3pm

DEGREE OF DIFFICULTY
Moderate

CONTACT
303.871.2000
www.du.edu

commencement ceremonies were on the lawn in front of the building, but this changed in 2001 when it moved to the Magness Arena.

One great story about the University of Denver occurred when student John Hall graduated. As he was the only student in that graduating class he designed this cheer: "Hear me roar, hear me roar. I'm the class of '84." The crowd cheered back "Hip, hip, hooray!"

The Penrose Library is another important stop. In addition to all the books you'd usually find in a library, this venue is filled with cookbooks, as well. The University of Denver has the second-largest cookbook collection, totaling more than 8,000, and some dating back 300 years. The number of volumes is impressive, especially considering the largest collection in the United States lives at the New York Public Library.

Other points of interest include the Buchtel Tower, the only remaining tower standing after the horrible fire of 1983. Also on the tour is the Ritchie Center, where students and community members use the fitness center and ice rink.

The tour will leave you with a lot of new information about this institution that so many Coloradoan's drive by daily. Not only are thousands of students pursuing their dreams here, but the University is also keeping the community history alive.

WYNKOOP BREWING COMPANY

The Wynkoop Brewing Company was the first brewpub established in Colorado, and they have sold enough beer to become one of the largest brewpubs in America. Quite impressive! The Wynkoop was named after Denver's first sheriff in 1858, Edward Wynkoop. As soon as you walk in the door, you will see the Barrel-o-Meter, which is a device that displays how much brew is produced in the facility.

The Wynkoop's menu features food that is to die for! They have one of the best hot artichoke and Parmesan cheese dip plates in the state, and it's even more perfect with a pint of brew. If you are looking for a superb meal, the shepherd's pie is one of the signature dishes that you can count on every time.

One of Wynkoop's most notable brews is the Railyard Ale, which was created for a wedding reception. The taste has a broad appeal and is one of the favorites at the brewery. Local promotion is a year-round affair, and often there are beer tastings held monthly to give the customers an opportunity to sample new recipes or old favorites. One of the highlight promotions is the National Finals of the Beerdrinker of the Year competition, for which the winner gets his or her weight in Railyard Ale.

LOCAL'S CHOICE: Patty's Chili Beer, which is a light golden ale with Anaheim peppers thrown in to give it some spunk.

TAKE THE TOUR

WHERE TO GO
1634 Eighteenth Street
Denver, CO 80202
WHEN TO GO
Guided Tour
Saturdays 1 – 3pm
DEGREE OF DIFFICULTY
Easy
CONTACT
303.297.2700
www.wynkoop.com

TAKE THE TOUR

WHERE TO GO
1000 Englewood Parkway
Suite 2-230
Englewood, CO 80110
WHEN TO GO
Self-Guided
Monday – Friday
8:30am – 5:30pm
DEGREE OF DIFFICULTY
Easy
CONTACT
303.806.0444
www.moaonline.org

MUSEUM OF OUTDOOR ARTS

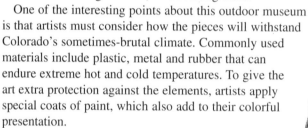

John W. Madden, Jr. and his daughter Cynthia Madden Leitner founded this museum in 1981 as a way to share art with the people working in the Greenwood Plaza Office Park. The official office of MOA is in the Englewood Civic Center, but pieces of art are also in the Lowery and Hudson gardens. One of the goals of the museum is to provide educational programs. Working with the community, MOA creates an opportunity for grade-school students to be involved in the arts.

The tour of the Museum of Outdoor Arts includes mostly experimental pieces, the majority of them displayed outdoors. The collection aims to expand our appreciation of the common workplace. Most of the exhibits concentrate on single artists, on a rotating basis.

One of the interesting points about this outdoor museum is that artists must consider how the pieces will withstand Colorado's sometimes-brutal climate. Commonly used materials include plastic, metal and rubber that can endure extreme hot and cold temperatures. To give the art extra protection against the elements, artists apply special coats of paint, which also add to their colorful presentation.

Some of the exhibits that you may enjoy include *The Horizon*, by Amy Langsen. Horses with wheels for feet stand in the middle of the grass. Another interesting exhibit is *The VW Bug*, painted in every possible color, in no particular pattern. It's an interesting look for a common vehicle.

Most of the outdoor exhibits rotate between the campuses, giving different communities the chance to see several pieces. The indoor gallery is on the second floor of the Civic Center, and includes pieces made from outdoor materials.

COLORADO SCHOOL OF MINES GEOLOGY MUSEUM

If you look out at the mountains and wonder how those big rocks came to be, you'll probably enjoy a visit to the Colorado School of Mines Geology Museum. It offers both guided and self-guided tours, so you can decide what's best for you and the kids. In any case, bring the kids, as they'll love this place, especially the segment of the museum designed with them in mind. More than 80 percent of the visitors at this museum are children, who love this adventure.

Starting as a teaching cabinet, assembled by Arthur Lakes in the 1870s, the museum was just a small collection of specimens. Over the years it has grown to include more than 60,000 minerals and 15,000 invertebrate fossils. The entire collection is known worldwide and you would be missing a great resource if you didn't tour it. The museum is planning a move during 2003, so expect to see some bigger and better exhibits once they get settled.

Your walk around the structured glass cabinets will give some insight into the

TAKE THE TOUR

WHERE TO GO
Colorado School of Mines
Department of Geology and
Geological Engineering
Golden, CO 80401

WHEN TO GO
Self Guided Tour
Monday - Saturday
9am – 4pm
Sunday 1pm – 4pm
Guided
Hourly
Reservations Required

DEGREE OF DIFFICULTY
Easy

CONTACT
303.273.3823 or
303.273.3815
**www.mines.edu/Academic/
geology/museum**

world of gems, minerals and geodes. The museum is divided into three sections: minerals of the world, invertebrate fossils and mining history. These aren't just ordinary rocks either: You are about to set your eyes on some fascinating discoveries in the world of geology.

Take, for example, the H.H. Nininger's meteorite collection. Mr. Nininger was one of the first great meteorite collectors, and in this collection you will see a 70-pound nickel-iron meteor, from the Meteor Crater in Arizona.

The Colorado Gem Trail case is another stop on your tour. This focuses solely on the minerals found in Colorado. Highlighting this section is the cleavelandite, from Florrisant, Colorado. There's also the Golden Area case, featuring specimens found within five miles of Golden. Toward the middle of the building is the entrance of the mine, so get ready to explore. This indoor, manmade mine is a great treat for those less likely to go underground. The lanterns hanging from the side of the walls make the experience seem real. The exhibit includes equipment that looks like it was left behind by miners who explored years ago. Also in the museum are examples of old drills, carts and mining equipment. These items offer perspective on hard this work must have been without electronic equipment.

COORS BREWERY

For one 125 years the Coors Brewing Company has considered Golden, Colorado, its hometown, although it's distributed worldwide. An opportunity to learn about the Rocky Mountain brewing tradition makes for an exciting tour.

When you arrive, park the car in the Coors visitor parking lot, which is located at 13th and Ford. Shuttle buses arrive every 15 -20 minutes, and they will take you to the main headquarters of Coors. You will also get a mini tour of Golden, as the bus drivers will point out interesting facts about the area and the city of Golden.

After exiting the bus, you will see the retired copper kettle, which is located in front of the building. It was one of the first copper kettles used in the Golden brewery and this is a great place to take a photograph of your group.

You will be greeted at the reception area inside the building. Tours are scheduled on a regular basis, but often the number of guests is a bit overwhelming, so Coors has come up with a great system. After arriving, you will be handed one of various Coors labels and you'll wait for your beer name to be called, in order to join a tour. While you're waiting you can walk around the visitor's center and view exhibits highlighting the history of Coors. You'll also learn why Adolph Coors chose this location for brewing in 1873.

TAKE THE TOUR

WHERE TO GO
13th and Ford Streets
Golden, CO 80401

WHEN TO GO
Guided Tour
Monday – Saturday
10am – 4pm
Tours leave from parking lot at
13th and Ford every 20 --30 minutes
Reservations Required for Groups of 20+
Ages: Under 18 years of age must be accompanied by an adult

DEGREE OF DIFFICULTY
Easy

CONTACT
303.277.BEER
www.coors.com

After your label name is called, the tour begins and you'll head toward the elevators. Getting to know more about the Coors tradition is an important aspect of this tour. It's the largest single-site brewery in the world and Coors has made its name through the high standards used in making their beers. Golden is known across America and perhaps around the world because of this standard of quality. One of the

stops on the tour is the Brewhouse with 50 copper brew kettles. The kettles are located on each side of the room and this is where the brewing process begins. Brewing mixture of barley malt and water are cooked together to form mash inside the brew kettles. Later in the process hops is added. Take note of the ingredients as you watch the initial stages of the process. Only Rocky Mountain water is used in the brewing! Coors purchases specially grown hops and they grow their own two-row barley, which helps them to keep a tight standard on the quality of the ingredients.

After the beer is brewed in the kettles it's filtered out, leaving a sweet liquid known as wort. Yeast is added to the wort and the fermentation process begins. The beer is transferred into tanks for the aging process. It stays in the tanks for six to eight weeks, which is longer than other large breweries. The aging process is an important aspect, as this delivers the full flavor and smooth taste -- A Coors tradition. Finally, the beer is cold-filtered in a sterile environment, in order to keep a brewery-fresh flavor.

The final stop of the tour is located near the packaging lines. Look down and you'll see the employees working with packages of Coors and preparing them for the stores. Coors transports all of their beer on refrigerated trucks and insulated railcars, which is a standard not found at any other brewery.

The tour officially ends in the packaging section, but you'll want to participate in the best part: the sampling room. Follow the crowd to the bar and you'll find a pleasant place to sit back and sample fresh-brewed Coors. The bartenders will provide tasting tips if you are looking for advice on a product that you've never sampled before, and they also offer non-alcohol drinks for your pleasure. After you're finished sampling, you might like to stop by the Coors shop to browse logo merchandise. The shop has plenty of Coors items available, as well as hard-to-find beer items.

Coors Brewing Company in Golden is a proud Colorado tradition, and the opportunity to discover how they brew their beers should not be missed!

GOLDEN PIONEER MUSEUM

During the early days of Colorado's settlement, it was a huge ordeal for pioneers to get into town and do their shopping. As years have passed, grocery stores, department stores, and malls have sprung up, and we've taken our conveniences for granted. Fortunately, the Golden Pioneer Museum has preserved the old-fashioned mercantile as reminder of bygone days. There are some great exhibits about Colorado, and good information about Golden's early days.

This self-guided tour is rich in historical information about the community and mining. You'll get a glimpse of a 19th-century hose cart – or fire truck --complete with a wrapped-up hose ready for the next fire. There are also instruments of yesteryear, including a velvet-covered piano that won a prize for design at the 1893 Columbian Exhibition in Chicago.

TAKE THE TOUR

WHERE TO GO
923 10th Street
Golden, Colorado
WHEN TO GO
Self-Guided Tour
Monday – Saturday
10am -- 4:30pm
DEGREE OF DIFFICULTY
Easy
CONTACT
303.278.7151
www.goldenpioneermuseum.com

The mercantile is the next stop. An entire store, historic cash register and all, is on display. Dry goods, bottles of supplies and all the necessities of the time are still "on sale." This collection is partially from a former grocer in Golden, Koenig's Grocery on Tenth and Washington. Other pieces came from pharmacies in Central City and Erie. When you walk by the exhibit, it's apparent how convenient our lives have become, compared to pioneer times. Also from this era is a slot machine, which you'll see on your way out of the museum. This simple contraption is a striking image of what you can find in Central City, today. The only recognizable difference is that this one has a worn handle.

Other exhibits include the Lois Elhers Indian Doll Collection, with dolls from 39 Native American tribes. Ms. Elhers, a schoolteacher, spent her summers traveling and collecting dolls while learning about the different Native American cultures.

Kids like the doll exhibit, but they're especially into the semi-permanent collection that highlights the jobs of the Golden Volunteer Fire Department, which has been active since 1873. Kids are welcome to grab a modern-day fire-fighting coat and hat to see how it feels to wear the gear. Hoses and information about fires are on display to help the youngsters understand what a serious job firefighting is.

LOOKOUT MOUNTAIN NATURE CENTER & PRESERVE

Learning about nature is the focus of this tour. The center is a place to enjoy the environment and learn from volunteers how nature works when humans aren't around to interfere.

The center, built in 1997, shows how eco-friendly materials can be recycled into useful matter. The wood floors are made from train boxcars, outdoor decking is made from soda bottles and the bathroom floor tiles are made from windshields. Looking closely you'll see that the floor, deck and tiles look like any other.

Inside, the interactive exhibits include a full-scale mountain lion ready to pounce on a deer, and a black bear looking for ants. In the corner, kids can enjoy the Discovery Room, where they can read books and play games. Use the binoculars in The Observation Room to see the surrounding landscape.

The land around the center is a 110-acre nature preserve donated by the Boettcher family, along with the historic Boettcher Mansion. The grounds are landscaped with native plants and have nearly two miles of nature trails. This includes an interactive trail that winds behind the building. The informational signs along the trail give a great description into the flora of the area.

TAKE THE TOUR

WHERE TO GO
910 Colorow Road
Golden, CO 80401
WHEN TO GO
Self-Guided Tour
Tuesday – Sunday
10am – 4pm
DEGREE OF DIFFICULTY
Moderate
CONTACT
303.526.0594
www.openspace.jeffco.us

NATIONAL EARTHQUAKE CENTER

TAKE THE TOUR

WHERE TO GO
1711 Illinois
School of Mines Campus
Golden, CO 80401
WHEN TO GO
Guided Tour
9am — 4pm
Reservations Required
DEGREE OF DIFFICULTY
Easy
CONTACT
303.273.8500
www.neic.cr.usgs.gov

The National Earthquake Information Center tracks and records earthquakes that take place around the world. Everyday, at least 50 earthquakes are recorded as they shake some part of the earth. Seismographs detect the vibrations of a quake, then measure and record them. On the third floor of the building you will see at least a dozen seismographs as they transmit information received from satellites. The severity of an earthquake is measured and its magnitude is recorded on a Richter scale, which was developed by Dr. Charles F. Richter.

A tour at the Information Center will give you a step-by-step account of what happens during an earthquake and how it changes our lives on earth. The tour guide will explain the details in the main room, where the seismographs are located. It might be a good idea to bring paper and a pen to jot down a few notes. On the south side of the room you will be able to look through a panel of glass and watch the scientists as they work. In 1997, this facility put together a program called: Recommended Provisions of the National Earthquake Hazards Reduction. It is a national program designed to help cities, counties and countries design better buildings and choose more appropriate areas for landfills, in order to prevent devastation if an earthquake does its shaking dance.

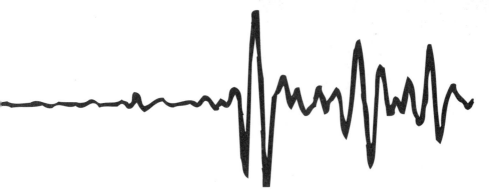

There are huge maps on the wall where you will see the Pacific Rim of Fire, better known to scientist as the place where many quakes happen consistently. You will see images of the California fault lines and maps provide detailed information about activities in other countries. For scientists, knowing where the plates are helps them accurately pinpoint where a quake might occur, which is especially important information for populated areas. Informative maps and satellites can also be viewed in the foyer and downstairs.

While in the main room, take a close look at the computer digital image located near the north wall. Here you will see information about the earthquakes that have been recorded in the last couple of hours. In 1882, an earthquake, which was a 6.6 on the Richter scale, was recorded just west of Fort Collins, making it the most severe earthquake to be documented in Colorado. Scientists have searched, but unfortunately never found the fault line of this particular event.

After completing the tour, you can stop by a small room located on the first floor, where you can overview the whole earthquake picture. You'll get better acquainted with the seismometer equipment, as you can jump near this machine and see the little meter interpreting the vibrations on paper. There is also free literature and neat postcards that the kids will love. If you do not have time for a guided tour, the downstairs facility is open every day and you can stop by without an appointment.

To help students, the National Earthquake Information Center offers a free packet that includes science experiments and detailed information.

NATIONAL RENEWABLE ENERGY LABORATORY

TAKE THE TOUR
WHERE TO GO
15013 Denver W. Parkway
Golden, CO 80401
WHEN TO GO
Self Guided Tour
Monday – Friday
8am – 5pm
Guided Tour
Monday – Friday
Reservations Required
DEGREE OF DIFFICULTY
Easy
CONTACT
303.384.6565
www.nrel.gov

The National Renewable Energy Laboratory, known as NREL, is located right off Interstate 70. At this facility they research, develop and improve ways to use renewable energy. The Solar Energy Research, Development and Demonstration Act established this sector of the government in 1974. While it has changed names over the years, the vision to use renewable resources for energy has remained the same.

What are renewable energies? Inside the visitor center there are displays explaining six important renewable energies: Solar, Wind, Ocean, Hydro, Biomass and Geothermal. These resources, when used in various ways, can save and produce energy in alternative ways. Renewable energy is important to create a healthier economy, a cleaner environment, and energy alternatives.

A tour at the visitor center will give you a basic understanding of how one can begin to utilize these six elements to save money and the precious environment. Just inside the door you will see a huge room filled with resourceful handouts. The handouts cover topics such as wind energy, bioenergy, as well as solar energy and its placement in homes, just to name a few. A small video room is also located in this area, where you can view videos on renewable energy and its importance in everyday life.

Down the hallway is a real wind turbine blade, which is 32 feet long and weighs close to 900 pounds. This advanced blade is an example of how we can capture energy that is renewable. NREL participates in the Colorado Windsource Program, which provides electricity to power this building. Large wind turbines, situated near the Wyoming border, generate electricity for the Windsource program.

Inside the gallery, you will learn about NREL's vision to empower America with energy choices. This exhibit, which uses a fictitious city, will give you the chance to see how one can maintain a high quality of life without destroying the natural resources. The interactive exhibits will keep you occupied and entertained for a while. You will also learn more about car pollution, and ways to minimize it. There is a computer-animated electric vehicle that children will love playing.

The first solar cells ever used were placed on a satellite, and enough power was generated by the sunlight to actually keep the machinery going. Using a makeshift roof, the exhibit "How Solar Electric Roofing Works" is an excellent place to see technology working in your own backyard. Solar cells make up shingles that are placed on top of the roof. While your roof is protected from outside elements, it also collects sunlight and creates enough electricity to live comfortably in your home.

The building that houses the visitor center utilizes a variety of renewable energy technologies, demonstrating how easy it can be to use this technology. An ancient technique, the Trombe wall is used to light and heat the exhibit hall, and motion sensors are placed near the exhibits to control the lights and the exit signs, which are illuminated by light-emitting diodes.

When you arrive at the visitor center kids can pick up a scavenger hunt worksheet and play a game that will help them better understand renewable resources. This is a tour for the whole family and it will give you ideas for remodeling your house, as well as help you better understand renewable energy and how to use our resources wisely.

CHOCOLATES BY MARY CAROL

TAKE THE TOUR

WHERE TO GO
2560 West Main
Littleton, CO 80120
WHEN TO GO
Guided Tour
Mothers Day – Labor Day
Reservations Required
DEGREE OF DIFFICULTY
Easy
CONTACT
303.795.7918
www.chocolatesbymary
carol.com

Chocolate-o-holics unite: This is one cool tour! Chocolates by Mary Carol is a small candy company with a big heart. During the candy-making off-season they open their doors so you can get a glimpse of chocolate heaven. Owners Ginny Gleason and Mary Carol started their company in 1979 in downtown Littleton. Focusing on premium chocolates with fresh ingredients, their business grew and has since become one of Colorado's signature, homegrown success stories.

The tour starts in the kitchen. Just to the left is the most important part of any chocolate tour -- the chocolate vat. Confectioners melt large bars of chocolate into a warm liquid, to ready the candy for its form. Some of the chocolate will be made into nut clusters, creams, and mints. Others will be fudge or even delicious molded chocolate pieces. According to locals, hand-dipped pieces are the specialty.

Once the chocolate is ready it is poured into molds. On my tour I saw several kinds of molds, including ones for the holiday season and for chocolate lollipops. The molds are filled to the top, and then set to cool on moving shelves. Once solid, the chocolate is carefully peeled out of the mold and decorated.

Decorating the pieces is as important as making the chocolate. Each piece is individually designed with eatable coloring and details that make the shapes come alive. On my tour, I watched a vat of dark liquid turn into a complex glittering chocolate sled.

It's also interesting to see how chocolate is packaged, which is done in several ways. Individual pieces are wrapped by hand, in foils placed around each piece and closed with precision. Chocolate assortments are boxed in special containers and, finally, holiday pieces are wrapped in clear bags.

The tour ends in the gift shop where you can purchase the handmade chocolates. There are also candy apples, jellybeans and a wide assortment of other treats. While I would love to tell you it is easy to walk away without spending a dime, you may find it difficult, as they all look so good!

DINOSAUR RIDGE

The world knows Morrison, Colorado, for its exceptional tracks -- dinosaur tracks that is. Today you will find the National Natural Landmark, Dinosaur Ridge, only 15 miles from downtown Denver. In 1877, Jurassic dinosaur bones from the Stegosaurus and Apatosaurus were found on the Ridge. These discoveries led scientists and laymen to look for and learn about the region's prehistory.

This is a tour for those who want to know about dinosaurs. The whole setup is family friendly and perfect for an afternoon of quality time. Do not forget to bring your camera for those snapshots next to the dinosaur bones or the comparison of dinosaur feet to your own. Dinosaur Ridge is a geological and paleontological (the study of life forms through fossils) outdoor museum.

A self-guided tour brochure can be picked up at the first stop on your tour, the Dinosaur Ridge Visitors Center. The Friends of the Dinosaur Ridge keep the Visitors Center open. You will be in good hands, as the 100 volunteers who staff the center are well versed in dinosaur facts and information. The goals of the association are to preserve and protect the resources on the Ridge, and to introduce and educate the public to the natural science.

At the Center you will be able to touch some of the fossils found on the Ridge, get answers to your pressing dinosaur questions and pick up a toy dinosaur for the kids at the souvenir store. You can also leave your car in the parking lot when you

TAKE THE TOUR

WHERE TO GO
16831 W. Alameda Parkway
Morrison, CO 80465

WHEN TO GO
Self-Guided Tour
Monday – Saturday
9am – 4pm
Sunday at Noon

DEGREE OF DIFFICULTY
Moderate

CONTACT
303.697.DINO
www.DinoRidge.org

begin your journey up the Ridge.

The Dinosaur Ridge trail is a two-mile stretch with dinosaur facts on markers placed next to each stop. The stops along the way give visual explanations of the prehistory of our land, long before Colorado became the frontier state. The private Rooney Ranch, homesteaded of the 1860s, is the newest landmark on the tour. Everything else on the tour dates back 100 million years with the Western Interior Seaway.

The dinosaur tracks are one of the highlights on the tour. You will be able to see over 300 footprints of the plant-eating and carnivore dinosaurs. This is where the kids get really excited so make sure the camera is out and ready.

Another highlight is the dinosaur bones at the end of the tour. This is the site of the 1877 discoveries of the Stegosaurs and his cousins.

You are welcome to visit and photograph all the fossils on the Ridge, but state law forbids collecting fossils. Preservation of the Ridge is important for future generations to see and explore.

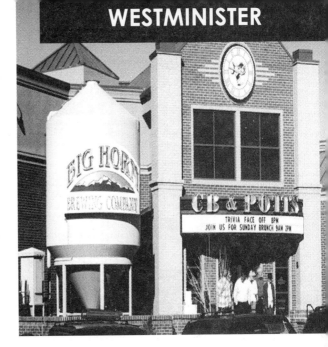

BIG HORN BREWERY

Despite the name, there are no big horn sheep at these two breweries. Instead, you are going to find some friendly folks who know their brews. The Big Horn Breweries are located inside the locally famous C.B. and Potts Restaurants.

The handcrafted beers are brewed at each location, respectively. The atmosphere found at both establishments is that of a cozy bar. While the brewery equipment is ready for your review on a pre-arranged tour, you will find that the brewers go all out in describing their process. Six different brews are available for your choice and they rotate four to five seasonal brews.

The food that accompanies your brews is American fare, featuring burgers, steaks, grilled chicken and other delicious entrees. I found this a great place to drop in and sip a pint.

LOCAL'S CHOICE: The Big Red Ale, which is a dark red ale with a bitter flavor. At the Westminster location, the brewery equipment can be seen from anywhere you sit, as it stands tall and proud. This location also has an impressive horseshoe bar, and if you want to check out a majestic sunset, you can take a break outside on the west patio.

TAKE THE TOUR

WHERE TO GO
1275 W. 120th Avenue
Westminster, CO 80234
43 W. Centennial Boulevard.
Highlands Ranch, CO 80129
WHEN TO GO
Guided Tour
2 – 4pm
Reservations Required
DEGREE OF DIFFICULTY
Easy
CONTACT
303.451.5767 (Westminster)
720.344.5767 (Highlands Ranch)

COLORADO

EATON

FORT COLLINS

LONGMONT

LOVELAND

LYONS

PAONIA

NORTHEAST

ANTIQUE WASHING MACHINE MUSEUM

If you have not yet met Lee Maxwell, you should. He lives and works just outside of Eaton, Colorado, and his claim to fame is that he's a washing machine connoisseur. In fact, he has hundreds of washing machines at his Antique Washing Machine Museum.

Washing machines have evolved over the years, from the washboards that pioneers used to clean clothes in rivers, to the super-duper machines we use today. As technology has advanced, so has the washing machine. From the diesel unit to the roller unit, you have to admit we have come along way in making our clothes look and feel clean.

The tour starts in the long barn that houses the machines. Lining the wall are washing machines, all in good condition and waiting for the next load. As you will see, most of the machines are dated so that it's easy to understand how technology has progressed over time. Don't worry if you become a bit overwhelmed, as Mr. Maxwell can give you endless details about the different models.

Now, I don't know about you, but I'm no expert on washing machines. So I'd like to share a few of my personal favorites with you and give you a glimpse of what to expect from this tour. There's this model produced by Almetal Manufacturing Company of St. Louis, Missouri, that's a washing machine that can also turn into a fruit and vegetable canner. Canning could only be done when the washer's inverted cone agitator was removed, making it impossible for the machine owner to wash and can at the same time. The machine held up to 32 quart jars in one canning batch. The washing machine function works like this: At the bottom of the machine is a copper kettle that heats the water, and a contraption that lifts the clothes out of the water as the lid opens. This was the only machine Almetal made

TAKE THE TOUR

WHERE TO GO
35901 WCR 31
Eaton, CO 80615
WHEN TO GO
Guided Tour
Reservations Required
DEGREE OF DIFFICULTY
Easy
CONTACT
970.454.1856
www.oldewash.com

and their slogan was "If men had to do the washing, every house would have an Almetal."

Another machine I was interested in is the Thor Washer, built in 1908. A wooden drum tumbles the clothes by rotating eight times in one direction, then reverses the cycle eight times. The wringer is controlled by pulling a lever on the side of the machine. Sadly, these machines could have caused serious injury if a finger, hair or body part got caught. The only way to stop the cycle was to unplug it. Also, dryers had not been invented this early in the 20th century.

In 1920 there were 1,300 companies producing washing machines. While you will only find 400 models at the museum in Eaton, it is safe to say you will see the gamut of the machines. From gas to electric, from pulleys to diesel, you can see how one might be fascinated by the history of the washing machines.

Mr. Maxwell does more than exhibit these priceless pieces; he actually dismantles, cleans, paints and reassembles each piece at his workshop (which you see on the tour). Every year he goes on hunts, searching for new pieces for his collection. He takes pleasure in sharing his treasures with other folks and does so with vigor and enthusiasm. Which goes to show it really doesn't matter what you collect as long as you enjoy collecting.

COLORADO STATE UNIVERSITY

The Agricultural College of Colorado was founded in 1870, but opened its doors to the public in 1879. President Elijah Edwards and two faculty members were the only teachers that year and the first class had five students. Today, Colorado State University (CSU) is a world-renown institution with 22,000 students and 1,400 faculty members.

The CSU tour begins at the Office of Admissions, in Spruce Hall. Anyone who wants to know more about the history of the state will enjoy this tour, which includes historical information about not only the institution but the community, as well.

TAKE THE TOUR

WHERE TO GO
Spruce Hall
Fort Collins, CO 80523

WHEN TO GO
Guided Tour
Monday – Friday
9:15 and 1:15
Saturday 9:15

DEGREE OF DIFFICULTY
Moderate

CONTACT
970.491.6909
www.colostate.edu

The tour begins with a walk around the campus's beautiful grounds. Usually guides are current students hoping to share information about their school. The heart of Colorado State University campus is the Oval, a grass commons with 65 American elm trees. The Administration Building, built in 1924, is on the south edge of the Oval and houses the office of the University's current president, as well as other offices of importance.

The Music Building, built in 1927, is next on the tour. Originally, the main library was situated here, but as the student body grew, so did the number of books. The library moved to another building and the Department of Music, Theater and Dance moved in.

The Lory Student Center, built in 1961 and named in honor of former CSU president Charles A. Lory, is another point of interest. This is the home of the student union and other student-led organizations.

Next to the Student Center is the Morgan Library, named after former CSU President William B. Morgan. This building was completed in 1964 and houses roughly two million volumes, to date.

This is an hour-long tour with moderate walking, so wear comfortable shoes to maximize your enjoyment as you make your way around the CSU campus.

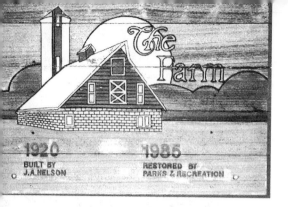

TAKE THE TOUR

WHERE TO GO
600 N. Sherwood Street
Fort Collins, CO 80521

WHEN TO GO
Self-Guided Tour
Wednesday – Saturday
10am – 4:30pm
Sunday noon – 4:30

DEGREE OF DIFFICULTY
Easy

CONTACT
970.221.6665

THE FARM AT LEE MARTINEZ PARK

The Farm at Lee Martinez Park is a glimpse of the country within the Fort Collins city limits. Not only does The Farm have the feel of a real rural setting, it's a great place to bring a picnic and enjoy the afternoon.

Originally, it was an operating dairy farm; the city of Fort Collins purchased this facility in 1973. It's an ideal place for families who are seeking a rural setting to teach children how animals are raised. The Farm has different areas to explore the lives of farm animals or just plain step away from the city life.

The barn that houses the cows is the first one on the right. The top of the barn is accessible by a stairway just inside the doors. Upstairs you can stroll across the walkway into the top portion of the silo, where you can view the entire farm. On the lower level, you can buy food for the animals in the Silo, and purchasing items at this store supports The Farm and the animals.

Geese are in the middle of the farm, next to a little pond. The horses live farther to the north of the barn and they might come up to the fence as you arrive. The pigs are a little bit dirty, as they have been rolling around in the mud. The goats, with their kids, are just west of the horses, and they seem to be enjoying themselves in the open pens. The final tour stop on the animal stroll is the chicken coop. The birds gather around the front and you will see roosters, fryers and Cornish hens.

The "North Forty Collection" is toward the northwest end of the property. Viewing the collection of older machinery, one will get an idea of the hard-working life that farmers had before commercial tractors were developed. The corn shellers and stock scales, plows and harrows, will likely pique your interest for farming in the early 1900's. There is a tractor situated in the playground area right around the corner, on which kids can climb and play.

When visiting The Farm, remember to stop by the Farm Heritage Museum, which focuses on how farmers and ranchers lived and worked the land. There are current agricultural and local farming facts, information that is often only shared within the agriculture community.

FACTS: 75-100 animals are adopted each year through monetary donations made by individuals in the community. The Farm was originally built by JA Nelson in 1920.

ODELL'S BREWING COMPANY

The Odell family founded their brewery in November of 1989, and they began bottling their beer in the spring of 1996. Odell's Brewing Company was the second microbrewery in Colorado and the first in Larimer County! The operation is family owned and when you walk into their facility you will know how proud they are of their brew.

Odell's Brewing specializes in English-style ales, using malt imported from Britain and hops from Washington State. The brewery produces 28,000 barrels annually, and they have a 60,000-barrel capacity in their new facility.

There is an elaborate gift shop, newly expanded to include seating for sample tasting. You'll have the opportunity to purchase all of the current beers, which are available in five different keg sizes or 12-ounce bottles. The brewery has a wide variety of logo merchandise, which includes items with the name of the brewery or the brew itself.

The walls of the gift shop are worth looking at, as they tell the story how brewmaster Doug Odell started his brewery. There are also pictures on the walls showing the construction of the facility and the different events Odell has participated in.

Odell's Brewing Company has a strong commitment to the brewing industry, and there is free information available, describing their beer-making process and the company history.

LOCAL'S CHOICE: 90 Shilling, a rich, smooth and satisfying amber ale. The name is from the Scottish method of naming beers for how much government tax is paid.

TAKE THE TOUR

WHERE TO GO
800 E. Lincoln Avenue
Fort Collins, CO 80524
WHEN TO GO
Guided Tour
Monday – Friday
10am – 3pm
Saturday 2pm
DEGREE OF DIFFICULTY
Easy
CONTACT
970.498.9070
www.odellbrewing.com

SWETSVILLE ZOO

TAKE THE TOUR

WHERE TO GO
4801 East Harmony
(Exit 265, off of I-25)
Fort Collins, CO 80521

WHEN TO GO
Self Guided Tour
Monday – Sunday
Dawn to Dusk

DEGREE OF DIFFICULTY
Easy

CONTACT
970.484.9509

A Tyrannosaurus Rex will be your official welcome to the Swetsville Zoo. Standing about two stories high, he is smiling and waving for you to come up and browse. Bill Swets, the artist and owner of the Swetsville Zoo, is modest about his amazing creations, which are sculptures made from various pieces of farm equipment and automotive parts. He has sculpted over 150 metal creations, which he displays throughout the area. Before beginning the tour, you can pick up a laminated guide that lists the names and corresponding numbers of the various zany sculptures.

Begin your exploration near the huge steel gates that lead you into the east garden, where the work is in a natural setting. A stone pathway takes you into the park, where flowers bloom on each side of the path and the grass is ever so green.

The pathway will guide you around the creations, and you will have the opportunity to view them close up. The creatures, as they are fondly referred to, are made

from leftover parts that have been welded together. One of my favorite exhibits along the path is the fly, with sink handles for eyes, but when viewed from far away they look like eyes of a monster. Another impressive exhibit is the big bug, made from a Volkswagen Bug body, with huge legs made out of pipes extending from underneath the shell.

When you see the Swets' house, you might think you're visiting a castle in Europe! The details are elaborate, including a special walkway surrounded by rocks, and flags flying from the rooftop.

You will also have the opportunity to view smaller zoo animals, which are located inside a The Bungled Jungle, a trailer that sits in front of the parking lot. Aliens, flowers, fish and much more are displayed! If you fall in love with a piece, you might have the chance to buy it from the Chrome Rose Gallery. As there are no lights in the trailer, it is a good idea to come during the brighter part of the day. The Swetsville Zoo is a great place to bring a picnic, and you can find a nice spot next to the pathway in the east garden. It's a perfect place to sit and relax, while viewing the zany creatures made by a guy who enjoys farming and living in Colorado.

TRANSFORT BUS SYSTEM

A tour at the Transfort Bus System, in Fort Collins, is a great place to teach children about alternative transportation and fuel conservation, and it will give them the opportunity to learn how to use the bus system. Transfort was established 26 years ago and the present facility is 17 years old.

Annually, they provide over a million rides, and college students along with those who are 17 and under always ride free!

The tour begins in the main building, and the guide will give an overview about the bus system and the training involved to be a bus driver. Currently, the Transfort System employs 80 bus drivers who cover the various routes including the Dial-A-Ride program. The tour proceeds to the bus yard, where the vehicles go when they are not in use, and the guide will explain some of the special features of the buses, including a demonstration of the wheelchair lift. One of the highlights of the tour is the mechanics center. Transfort employs in-house mechanics who work exclusively with the buses. The next portion of the tour includes an opportunity to ride a bus, and the tour guide will explain the importance of safety on a moving vehicle. During the ride, the guide will explain the various procedures of bus riding and they will answer any questions about the Transfort Bus System. Before returning to the main building, the bus goes through the bus wash, and you will be given a bus schedule for future use. Transfort hopes to encourage families to use the alternative transportation by giving out free-ride coupons at the end of the tour.

VERN'S TOFFEE HOUSE

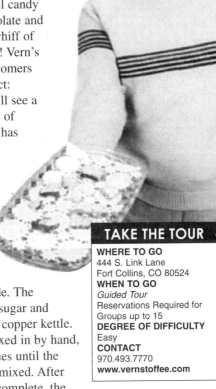

Vern's Toffee House produces a delightful candy creation combining the best almonds, chocolate and butter. They are open year-round and one whiff of the candy will stop you right in your tracks! Vern's was founded in 1976, and they cater to customers around the world with one exclusive product: toffee. Just inside the main entrance you will see a map that is covered with colored pins, each of which represents a Vern's customer. Toffee has been shipped to the Vatican, Ireland, Singapore, Bolivia and almost everywhere else you can imagine! The company produces 25,000 - 30,000 pounds of toffee annually and this number will continuously increase as more people discover one of Colorado's best-kept secrets.

A tour of the factory will give you an excellent overview of how toffee is made. The procedure begins with a mixture of butter, sugar and water, which is stirred as it heats in a large copper kettle. Whole almonds are mixed in by hand, and the stirring continues until the ingredients are evenly mixed. After the heating process is complete, the toffee is poured on to a specially designed water-cooled steel table. Moving the kettle requires two people, as it is extremely heavy. The hot mixture is spread evenly across the table and a layer of melted milk chocolate, along with a blanket of crushed raw almonds, is spread on top of the toffee. The toffee is turned over so the chocolate-and-almond process can be repeated, after which it is moved to the cooling trays. A tray of toffee weighs about 45 pounds, and once it is cooled, the toffee is cut and put into one- or two-pound packages. It is clear to see that the employees of Vern's Toffee House proudly make each piece of toffee!

The secret recipe is the creation of Vern Hackbarth, who retired from the restaurant business in 1976 and decided to mass-produce his toffee. The venture was so successful that he asked his daughter Mary and her spouse Ron Hert to join the company. Today Mary and Ron own the company and Vern has retired once again.

TAKE THE TOUR

WHERE TO GO
444 S. Link Lane
Fort Collins, CO 80524
WHEN TO GO
Guided Tour
Reservations Required for Groups up to 15
DEGREE OF DIFFICULTY
Easy
CONTACT
970.493.7770
www.vernstoffee.com

FORT MORGAN MUSEUM

Fort Morgan has a special hometown boy – bandleader Glenn Miller. The Fort Morgan High School graduate is one of the town's best-known residents to hit stardom. The museum tour highlights this famous man's life, in addition to important details about the history and culture of this town.

The Glenn Miller exhibit shows what a regular "Joe" he was before RCA awarded him the first gold record in history. Miller sold over 1,200,000 copies of the "Chattanooga Choo Choo" album, and was also locally famed for his role as Left End on the high school football team. In 1920, he was named "Best Left End in Colorado." On this tour you'll learn that Miller's love for music was influenced by Elmer Wells, an orchestra director who asked Glenn to sit in with his band. This experience ignited a flame for Miller, and he eventually began his own band. Years of performing paid off for him, as he is regarded as the most popular Big Band leader in the era of Big Bands.

The historical part of the Fort Morgan Museum tour begins at the Old Hillrose Soda Fountain, where you can almost imagine a soda hopper would be right behind the counter, taking your order for a chocolate soda or ice cream treat. The counter comes equipped with the old-fashioned cash register and Coca-Cola memorabilia.

The Fort Morgan Military Fort is also a highlight. From 1864 until 1868, it housed military men who guarded the plains and kept the peace. Uniforms are on display, as well as the men's "basics," including a fork, spoon, gun, and cup.

Since agriculture and farming have been staples of the area, today and in years past, it makes sense that the farming exhibit would detail the evolution of agricultural equipment. A hand plow gives some idea of how much work it really took to plow a field, before the advent of motorized tractors. Photographs are part of the exhibit, showing community members working the land.

Steps away from the farming exhibit is a 12,000-year-old horse skull. Found during a museum excavation, this interesting artifact is the only one known in Colorado. Don't miss it!

TAKE THE TOUR

WHERE TO GO
414 Main Street
Fort Morgan, CO 80701

WHEN TO GO
Self-Guided
Monday – Friday
10am – 5pm
Saturday
11am – 5pm
Tuesday – Thursday
6 – 8pm

DEGREE OF DIFFICULTY
Easy

CONTACT
970.867.6331
www.ftmorganmus.org

MEEKER HOME

TAKE THE TOUR
WHERE TO GO
1324 9th Avenue
Greeley, CO 80631
WHEN TO GO
Guided Tour
Mid-April – Mid-October
Tuesday – Saturday
10am – 3pm
DEGREE OF DIFFICULTY
Easy
CONTACT
970.350.9220
www.greeleymuseums.com

If you want to see an eloquent 1870s residence, visit Greeley's Meeker Home, where you'll get historical background about the city and its founder.

Nathan Meeker, who was an agriculture editor for the New York Tribune, was friends with Horace Greeley and came here on a mission to organize a model city in the West. His plan was to persuade people in diverse professions to move here and contribute funds toward the development of a cooperative community.

In 1870, the first Union Colonist arrived by train and settled down to live. In only a year the town was considered a success, with 1,500 people and miles of land being used. The town flourished, but Nathan Meeker's income dwindled. He took a job as Indian Agent on the Western Slope and was killed in the 1879 White River Massacre.

The sidewalks along the home are lined with interpretive panels that discuss the region and history of the home. In 1929, the city purchased Greeley's first museum to share the history with everyone. Guides give individuals (groups are charged a tour fee) interesting descriptions of how the family lived and worked within the home. Several pieces of furniture inside the home belonged to the Meeker family, and others are replicas, showing the comfortable lifestyle the family enjoyed from 1890 until 1905.

When Nathan Meeker was killed, the women of the family struggled to make ends meet. Part of the tour focuses on how they survived living in this new colony.

There are benches, trees and lush grass surrounding the home, so give yourself a little extra time to sit outside and relax.

UNIVERSITY OF NORTHERN COLORADO

In the middle of Greeley, students scurry around, attending classes at the University of Northern Colorado. Smaller than Colorado State University or University of Colorado, it can provide an intimate college atmosphere, but still offer the advantages of larger schools. Approximately 11,000 students walk the campus daily. They come from 47 states and 52 nations around the world. The roots of the university have been in the Weld County area since 1890 and they are proud to be part of this community and the global community, as well. The University of Northern Colorado tour is rich with history and tidbits. Don't think this is designed for prospective students only.

The tour starts at the visitor center, which was the former residence of the presidents of UNC from 1924 until 1999. After a brief session on school life, the tour heads out to explore the campus. On April 1, 1989, the governor of Colorado signed a bill allowing the State Normal School to start training teachers. After changing names a couple of times, the school became University of Northern Colorado.

As you walk by the University Center, imagine what it looked like years ago. On the grounds of the Petrikin Farm, the building actually sits where the house once stood. The center is the main place where students enjoy a cup of coffee or check their email.

Don't forget to take a minute to look inside the Michener Library, dedicated in 1971. One of the well known facts about the campus is the James A. Michener Special Collection. The famous author and 1937 alumni donated the collection, which includes research materials, personal papers and manuscripts all related to the book Centennial. Also included in this collection are assorted mementos he collected over the years.

Expect the tour to take a solid hour and wear comfortable shoes so you can walk about with ease.

TAKE THE TOUR

WHERE TO GO
501 20th Street
Greeley, Colorado 80639

WHEN TO GO
Guided Tour
Reservations Required

DEGREE OF DIFFICULTY
Moderate

CONTACT
970.351.1890
www.unco.edu

CHEESE IMPORTERS

Cheese is one thing that is universal in our world, and you can find the best European and Domestic cheeses in the 5,000-square-foot cooler located at the Cheese Importers. It's the only place in the state that has such a unique cheese opportunity, and I encourage everyone who loves cheese to check out the tour.

For the most part, the tour of the Cheese Importers company takes place in the cooler. You can't miss the cooler, as it's only about 10 paces inside the door, to the right. Before you begin, I must warn you that once you step inside there is no turning back: You'll be immediately seduced by the sights and smells surrounding you.

This is a direct importer, with exceptional quality cheeses, organized by country and type. At the beginning of the tour, the guide will point out the more obscure types, such as local goat cheese and softer cheeses that might be mistaken for sour cream. Also, in the front of the cooler are sticks of meat, pate and other gourmet foods that are not usually found at retail outlets.

There are five aisles of cheese, and the 20-minute tour will give you the opportunity to learn about cheese with flavors from around the world. Cheddar, Gouda, Colby, pepper jack, Edam and mozzarella adorn the shelves in the first couple of aisles. Farther back are mellower cheeses such as Swiss, havarti, brick and string. Don't walk too fast or you might miss the endcaps, which feature information about cheese as well as suggestions for fancy dishes that can be made. The cheese doesn't stop there either: There's also Amish blue cheese, gorgonzola, monastery, Roquefort, provolone, blue cheese, asiago and mascarpone.

TAKE THE TOUR

WHERE TO GO
33 S. Pratt Parkway
Longmont, CO 80501

WHEN TO GO
*Guided and
Self Guided Tours*
Monday – Friday
9am – 6pm
Saturday
9am – 5pm
Sunday 11am – 4pm
Reservations Required for
Guided Tours

DEGREE OF DIFFICULTY
Easy

CONTACT
303.772.9599
www.cheeseimporters.com

If you have the time, take a minute to smell the individual cheese packages. You will notice the distinctive flavors and feel the texture and firmness of the cheese. Additionally, the Cheese Importer folks are kind enough to offer cheese and crackers for sampling. The types of cheeses available will rotate, so you might have the opportunity to try something completely new to your palate.

As a direct importer, they receive many whole wheels of cheese. While the shelves are partially filled with cut cheese, you can see the wheels and bricks in the back, waiting to be cut. Some of the wheels weigh as much as 500 pounds, and are the size of a tire.

The closed coolers feature another important aspect of cheese: cheesecake! Other products are noodles with cheese and foods that compliment cheese, as well.

After touring the cooler, you will be able to visit a little room that is located next to the exit. This is where they slice the cheese and wrap it for distribution. I have been there several times to watch them cut the wheels into pieces. The cutting process is an art, as they take their time to make each cut perfect.

Near the cooler, there is a small shop selling gift items and the Cheese Importer's free handout about cheese-eating as an art. If you enjoy olives or olive oil, the olive bar is another stop that I recommend making before leaving the building. The shop features an extensive collection of both. The containers of the olive oil are as elaborate as the oil itself, and they would be beautiful to display in your kitchen.

LEFTHAND TABERNASH BREW CO.

The Lefthand and Tabernash breweries merged in 1998, to better serve their customers and provide brews in a bottle for all of Colorado to enjoy. The brewery is a little off the beaten track, but you'll know you've arrived when you see the huge red hand that is painted on their silo!

Due to safety measures, the tour runs on a schedule, and guests are only permitted during designated times. Weekends are a good time to visit, although you will not see the bottling line moving.

Upon entering the building, you will notice the nice gift shop (open during business hours), offering logo merchandise. This is an elaborate shop, with t-shirts, caps and cycling jerseys with the Lefthand logo, and my favorite – the free bottle crown magnets. They are a cool reminder of which beer you love and what it looks like. If that is not enough, they have beer that you can take home.

LOCAL'S CHOICE: Sawtooth Ale is extremely popular, constituting 55% of Lefthand- Tabernash's sales. It is an amber ale, extra special bitter, very well balanced, with both hop and malt character.

TAKE THE TOUR

WHERE TO GO
1265 Boston Ave.
Longmont, CO 80501
WHEN TO GO
Guided Tour
Saturday 10am - 4:30pm
DEGREE OF DIFFICULTY
Easy
CONTACT
303.772.0258
www.lefthandbrewing.com

OSKAR BLUES GRILL AND BREW

TAKE THE TOUR

WHERE TO GO
303 Main Street
Lyons, CO 80540
WHEN TO GO
Guided Tour
Monday – Friday
9am – 5pm
Reservations Required for
Large Groups
DEGREE OF DIFFICULTY
Easy
CONTACT
303.823.6685
www.oskarblues.com

If you're looking for the perfect blues-brewery, you'll need to head out to Lyons. Oskar Blues Grill and Brew is a one-of-a-kind Colorado brewery that serves up great brews and live blues. Stepping into the building, you might think you missed a turn and dropped into a famous blues club in Chicago. Photographs of famous blues artists and musicians who have played live shows here line the walls.

And the food in the restaurant is just as hot as the music! There is a huge selection that caters to any taste, but if you're into Cajun-style food you're in luck! From jambalaya to gumbo, the restaurant provides a mouthful, and the beer is high quality, as well. Using a seven-barrel system, the brewmaster pays close attention to his five scrumptious brews. The redwood room and the hand-crafted brewing equipment work together to create a wonderful atmosphere. Eight beers are available at Oskar's, and are distributed to three restaurants on the Pearl Street Mall in Boulder.

Before you leave, look at the display of bottle crowns. Keeping with the spirit of brews, there is a floor-to-ceiling column of bottle crowns - a memorial to brews that were consumed while listening to the blues.

LOCAL'S CHOICE: Dale's Pale Ale, a hoppy American Pale as big as the Colorado sky.

TERROR CREEK WINERY

Terror Creek Winery, named after the snow-fed creek that tumbles along the winery's property, overlooks the North Fork Valley from Garvin Mesa, and the drive out to the winery is delightful! A visit to their tasting room will give you the opportunity to savor the delicious wines of the establishment. Wine bottles displayed in the tasting room give you a chance to look over the choices, and you can relax in the alpine garden that overlooks the vineyard.

John and Joan Mathewson, winery owners, have created Swiss and Alsatian-style wines that are a specialty in the Western Slope area. The vintner, Joan, was Swiss-trained, and she strives to develop a selection of wines that come alive with fruit flavor and crisp acidity.

The Terror Creek Winery is small but they are one of the best family-owned wineries in Colorado. If you're interested in visiting the winery, call in advance so they will know you're on the way!

TAKE THE TOUR

WHERE TO GO
1750 4175 Drive
Paonia, CO 81428

WHEN TO GO
Self-Guided Tour
Tasting Room Hours:
Memorial Day – Labor Day
11am – 5pm
Or by Appointment

CONTACT
970.527.3484

COLORADO

CANON CITY

COLORADO SPRINGS

PUEBLO

HISTORIC DOWNTOWN CANON CITY WALKING TOUR

If you get down to Royal Gorge, then you can't miss Canon City. In 1862 it was designated the county seat of Fremont County. Its name came from the close proximity of the town to the Grand Canyon of the Arkansas River. In 1895 the town flourished, due to the gold strikes in nearby South Park and California Gulch. The first territorial prison was constructed at the foot of the Dakota Hogback in 1871 and a year later, the town was incorporated by Mayor George Rockafellow.

The downtown portion of Canon City is roughly 80 structures, built in the late 19th and early 20th centuries. Most are two-story, brick buildings that follow a variety of popular 20th-century architectural styles, including Classical and Renaissance revivals. Only a block off highway 50, the Main Street is the historical commercial core of the community.

From Third to Eighth streets, you'll pass many fine architectural examples of the era. Some highlights include Raynolds Bank and McGee Building. An example of Gothic Revival, the building is a pinkish color built with stone shipped from Castle Rock. The reason the building has two names is most interesting: Payment to build the building was made by Fred A. Raynolds who financed the east half and W.B. McGee who financed the west half. You can see the building from the corner of Third Street.

The St. Cloud Hotel, on Sixth and Main Street, is also of interest. This four-story building was constructed in 1879 in Silver Cliff. From 1883 until 1886 it was moved brick by brick to Canon City and reconstructed. There are also four active historic churches within a five-block area. The First Baptist Church, dedicated in 1892, is on Seventh Street and was the first church in the area. The building is made out of Harding red sand stone.

The Chamber of Commerce offers a walking tour brochure of Canon City. It has great descriptions and historic photographs, and the pamphlet makes a nice souvenir of your adventure.

TAKE THE TOUR

WHERE TO GO
Canon City Chamber of Commerce
403 Royal Gorge Boulevard..
Canon City, CO 81212

WHEN TO GO
Self Guided
Daily

DEGREE OF DIFFICULTY
Easy

CONTACT
719.275.2331
www.canoncitychamber.com

AMERICAN NUMISMATIC ASSOCIATION MONEY MUSEUM

TAKE THE TOUR

WHERE TO GO
818 N. Cascade Ave.
Colorado Springs, CO
80903

WHEN TO GO
Self-Guided Tour
(group tours available)
Monday – Friday
9am – 4pm
Saturday
10am – 4pm

DEGREE OF DIFFICULTY
Easy

CONTACT
719.632.COIN
www.money.org

Since the creation of money nearly 3,000 years ago, coins have not only served to facilitate commerce but they also tell stories of people and nations. Today, coin collectors (numismatists) will tell you that holding old money in your hand can be magical, transporting you to distant parts of the world and eras long past. But you don't need to be a collector to travel with the ANA's Money Museum.

Recently remodeled, the Money Museum offers an ever-changing array of exhibits designed to appeal to a wide variety of interests, including history, art, archaeology, banking and economics, as well as to dazzle the senses with what money has been, is today and can be tomorrow. There's always something to see in the museum's contemporary galleries. The 5,000-square-foot Main Gallery features a new exhibit every year, as well as the "Minting Gallery" that showcases the United States Mint's first steam-powered press and other minting equipment. The 3,000-square-foot Lower Gallery presents new exhibits every four months and includes a component devoted to the history of Colorado Springs and the Pikes Peak Region.

On permanent display are the finest specimens from the most comprehensive collection of America's gold coins – assembled by the late Harry W. Bass Jr., who once managed the Vail ski resort and developed Beaver Creek ski resort. The 500-plus piece collection of gold coins, coin "patterns" and paper money, valued at more than $20 million, features material that traces the history of America. Visitors walk through massive, bronzed steel gates – emblazoned with United States Treasury Seals – into a warm and richly paneled exhibit area, where they can experience the audio- and computer-enhanced displays that tell the story of America's gold coins and the nation. Fiber-optic lighting illuminates the material, while a touch of a button cues descriptive narrations by former U.S. Mint Director Jay W. Johnson. A panorama of images encircle the room, illustrating the history of America's money, the story of gold, the mints and minting process, and the work of engravers.

The ANA's comparative collection of numismatic material is considered one of the world's finest. The Money Museum houses more than 300,000 coins, medals, tokens and pieces of paper money, a collection that grows constantly through donations, bequests and funded purchases. The collection includes coins from all countries through the ages and "primitive money" used in commerce by early cultures.

Visitors are welcomed six days a week (seven days in the summer), with free group tours available. At the end of your visit, children can grab one of the free foreign coins from the treasure chest in the reception area.

BEAR CREEK NATURE CENTER

TAKE THE TOUR

WHERE TO GO
245 Bear Creek Road
Colorado Springs, CO

WHEN TO GO
Self-Guided Tour
Tuesday – Saturday
9am – 4pm

DEGREE OF DIFFICULTY
Easy

CONTACT
719.520.6387
www.elpasoco.com/parks/
nature/nature.asp.

Opened in 1976, the Bear Creek Nature Center – then called the Solar Trails Center – was Colorado's first facility of its kind. It's purpose was to teach the public about nature on a local level but, tragically, a fire that started in an outdoor trashcan destroyed the building. With the community's help, the Bear Creek Nature Center opened to the public in May 2000. The new open-air building best reflects the center's role in the community: a window to nature.

In one corner, a stuffed bird hangs from the ceiling, as if it's watching you as its prey. Stand underneath and spread your arms out to get an idea of this creature's three-foot wingspan. The bear skull is also a reminder of how large these animals get, and how important it is for humans to respect the bear's habitat.

Kids are invited to feel bear and coyote fur or play nature trivia games on the computer. There is also a place where you can listen to bird calls, bat noises and bear growls. If bees are interesting to you, the honeycomb exhibit is a must-see: Bees enter the exhibit from the outside of the building through a clear plastic tube. The center also has a native bug display with insects collected from the Bear Creek Trails. The natural shrubs camouflage many of the bugs, so you have to look closely to see all the species.

Helping people to keep in touch with nature in this crazy world is one of the goals of the center. You'll learn how to act if you should come face-to-face with animals, and how to keep those pesky raccoons out of the trashcans. After the tour of the center, head outside to enjoy the trails.

BRISTOL BREWING COMPANY

Walking into the Bristol Brewing Company is like walking into a 1950's bus terminal. Inside the door there is an old-fashioned telephone booth, and nearby is a string of chairs, just like the ones at a bus stop. If you are looking for a place to have a pint, get a sample or learn more about the brewing process, you've come to the right place! If you have a favorite Bristol brew, or you especially like one of the label designs, there are plenty of shirts to choose from with the beer logos.

The Bristol Brewing Company is a microbrewery, so more than half of the area is filled with brewing equipment. You can see most of it by looking through the window, but by all means go in and ask about setting up a tour. Founded in June 1994, the company has become a mainstay in the community, and offers a steady stream of six brews. Their mission is to make beer that brings three things together: quality, purity and sanity. They use only natural ingredients and distribute locally, only a few miles from where you sit and sip. Located on the far wall are kegs and jugs ready for purchase, just waiting for the perfect customer to walk through the door.

LOCAL'S CHOICE: The Mass Transit, which is a smooth, mellow ale with a label sporting a VW Bus.

COLORADO SPRINGS PIONEERS MUSEUM

A few blocks from downtown is the tour at the Colorado Springs Pioneers Museum, with great information about the history of Pikes Peak. The museum is on two floors, in the El Paso County Courthouse, built in 1903. Included in the tour is an opportunity to walk into one of the courtrooms on the second floor, left as it was before the court moved to the new buildings.

The friendly museum staff will greet you as you walk up the steps and through the door. Take a map, and head for the toy room. Here you'll see how toys have evolved. Older toys were more functional, including items such as sewing and baking machines. In any case, you'll see the toys on display have all been worn with love! Suspended from the ceiling are a classic red wagon and an old-fashioned tricycle. Next to the toy room are exhibit halls highlighting the history of the area and including rotating exhibits.

To get to the second floor, you could take the stairs on either side of the room or, better yet, take the birdcage elevator. Although the lever doesn't rotate anymore,

you can push the button for the second floor. The kids will definitely enjoy the ride!

Upstairs, the "Health in the Pike's Peak Area" exhibit is something to see. While the sign on W.L. Bartlett and Co. Dentists Offices says they will help get you a great smile, you have to wonder about the instruments displayed on the table. After viewing these, you'll realize how much technology has helped the medical world to develop. Next to the dentist office you'll see instruments used for eye exams and by doctors making house calls. Local physicians helping people in the Pikes Peak community used all of the equipment on display.

On the other side of the building is the House of Helen Hunt. Ms. Hunt was a famous author and a noted literary figure who was nationally published. The remainder of the exhibit covers the people who lived in the Pikes Peak area including Native Americans.

Return to the first floor to explore the gift shop and to check out the beautiful structure of the building.

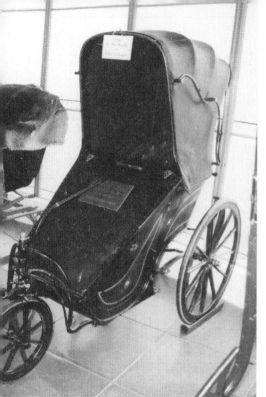

EL POMAR CARRIAGE HOUSE

In this great land of SUVs, it's hard to believe that cars weren't always our mode of transportation. Before the fast-paced freeways, the best means of getting from here to there was by carriage. Pulled by mules or horses, carriages took people around at a much slower pace and were a lot less comfortable than cars. The tour at the El Pomar Carriage House gives an idea of what transportation was like years ago.

When Spencer Penrose, owner of the Broadmoor, died in 1939 his spouse Julie collected carriages from friends and family across the United States, and brought them together at this museum.

The museum holds 33 carriages, most of which have been traced back in history. U.S. Several belonged to presidents, including an 1862 C-Spring Victoria, pulled by two horses and owned by the 21st president, Chester A. Arthur.

The well-kept Gentleman's Drag is one of the fancier models displayed here. Used for social outings in the country, it could carry up to 15 people. Along with those people aboard, there was an icebox in the back for picnic perishables, room for the plates, crystal and utensils. Four horses pulled the entire carriage.

The covered Conestoga wagon, located on the far wall of the museum, was made in Pennsylvania. Pulled by four or six oxen, its family traveled the country in it during the California Gold Rush. The wheels of the wagon are made of wood, offering little buffer for every bounce and bump felt along the way. The pioneers had fragile valuables including crystal, so to keep them safe, they would pack the items in wooden barrels full of flour.

The museum also houses a nice collection of saddles, including one for women, a polo game, and even one for Mongolian soldiers. A roulette table from a casino that once stood in the Broadmoor is also on display. The casino, which burnt down, was a popular place among the locals.

Impromptu tours sometimes happen at this museum. The three staff people are a wealth of information and really know the history of yesteryear.

FOCUS ON THE FAMILY

There are over 75 different religious organizations in Colorado Springs, and one of the largest is Focus on the Family. Their mission is to help preserve the traditional family values, based on scripture from the Bible.

TAKE THE TOUR

WHERE TO GO
8655 Explorer Drive
Colorado Springs, CO 80920

WHEN TO GO
Administration Guided Tour
Monday – Saturday
9am-noon; 1-4pm

DEGREE OF DIFFICULTY
Easy

CONTACT
800.AFAMILY
www.family.org

The founder of Focus on the Family, Mr. James Dobson, started the organization in 1977 with a 25-minute radio program. He continued that program and there was a daily broadcast to 4,000 facilities in 1999. Now the show is translated in different languages, reaching people of various nations. Focus on the Family also publishes 10 magazines, with a readership of 2.3 million people every month. Additionally, they have a catalog of books and pamphlets distributed to those in need of spiritual counseling.

The building is huge, housing most of the 1,300 employees and 300 - 400 volunteers working with the ministry.

The tour group gathers at the front reception and departs on the hour. The guide will explain some of the facts and figures regarding the organization, and after briefly answering questions will begin to acquaint you with Focus on the Family.

When you see the immaculate staircase leading to an area known as Main Street you will understand why the ministry appropriately named the steps "Little Pikes Peak." On the walls are awards that the ministry has won for their children's programming, as well charts and information about how this organization touches the lives of people around the world. Your tour guide will stop at each display and enlighten you on how the information fits into the big plan at Focus on the Family.

The correspondence department is the first room you will visit, and it is the heart of the ministry. Here are people who respond to 1,000 pieces of mail every day. Many of the letters need personal responses while others are requests for information or pamphlets. On the way out of the room, heading back towards Main Street, you will see all the honorary degrees Mr. Dobson has earned over the last 20 years.

At the end of Main Street you will see the Chapeleria room, used as a dining area for employees and an auditorium when the employees gather once a month for chapel service.

You'll then head back down Little Pikes Peak, and into the gallery, where the audience sits while listening to Dr. Dobson radio program. The control room is on the right side of the studio and you can glimpse the sound and recording equipment. After the tour is completed, you can help yourself to the different magazines and information available about Focus on the Family.

FOCUS ON THE FAMILY WELCOME CENTER

TAKE THE TOUR

WHERE TO GO
8650 Explorer Dr.
Colorado Springs, CO 80920

WHEN TO GO
Self-Guided Tour
Welcome Center and
Campus
Monday – Friday
9am – 5pm
Saturday
9am – 4pm
Summer
Monday – Friday
9am – 5pm
Saturday
9am – 5:30

DEGREE OF DIFFICULTY
Easy

CONTACT
719.531.3400
www.fotf.org

Don't be surprised if you are greeted at the door of Focus on the Family's Welcome Center. This is a friendly bunch of folks wanting you to enjoy what they have to offer. Focus on the Family is a ministry based in Colorado Springs. Their ministry is to help preserve traditional family values, based on scripture from the Bible. The Welcome Center tour will give you an overview on how the ministry works.

Over 70 ministries make up the organization, but Focus on the Family is widely known for the broadcast of Dr. James Dobson. Interactive displays are user friendly for children and adults. Posted on the wall is a step-by-step guide on how the broadcast is produced.

On the gallery floor, you will hear the noise coming from a special slide called the A-Bend-A-Go. Three stories high, it twists and turns dropping down into the Kid's Korner, which is the perfect place to spend time with the family. There is a B-17 Bomber replica and a lifelike mine, which will give you the chance to see what mining was like in the golden days. The video-viewing corral is right around the corner, and the entire area is a great place for the young ones to explore.

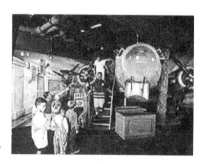

You can also visit the Whit's End Soda Fountain, which is a step back in time to the turn of the 20th century. Here you can buy fun treats at reasonable prices. Follow the signs upstairs to find the bookstore, which is close to the entrance. There is a large selection of religious materials and logo merchandise available, so you might find what you are looking for. After shopping you can take a minute to glance at the complimentary periodicals that are available for you to take home.

GARDEN OF THE GODS VISITOR CENTER

The name "Garden of the Gods" was given to the park in 1859. Rufus Cable, one of the two surveyors who came upon the sandstone formations said "Why it is a fit place for the Gods to Assemble." And so it has been called ever since. If you have never seen the area before, you'll be taken by the gorgeous sandstone rock formations jutting into the sky and imposing upon the landscape. It's very different scenery, compared to the mountains and formations only a few miles away. The Visitor Center is across the street from the park entrance. Not only does it offer a great view of what you'll see in the park, but it provides a chance to know a little more about the area's history.

One the first floor there is an introduction to the animals of the region. Several life-size buffalo stare you down as you walk in the door. Information on how the people of the land lived and ate these animals are on display. Just before the stairs, there is a neat exhibit on native Colorado grasses. It provides information on the four types that grow wild in the state, including buffalo grass.

As you head upstairs, you'll see a life-size big horn sheep. There's also a plethora of large, old photographs collected from past visitors. Stuffed birds are here, too as well as dinosaurs, on the north side. Of course, the dinosaurs are the kids favorite stop. Luckily, these creatures didn't damage the formations at the park, but they could have with their big feet! Their mommies must have taught them to watch where they walk.

The second-floor foyer is a rotunda-shaped area with artists' renderings of how the land must have looked thousands of years ago. Looking through the doors from here, you can see the beauty of the park. Go outside to feel the wind and take in the intense surroundings. Using the park as a backdrop, visitors often line up on the balcony to get their picture taken. A sandstone slab carved with the words "Garden of the Gods" makes this the perfect photo-op.

Once you've finished touring the center, you need to get to the park. Depending on how much time you have and your desire, you can hike, walk, or drive through. A map is available at the center's main desk, and don't forget the park provides daily guided nature walks. Times are posted at the visitor center.

TAKE THE TOUR

WHERE TO GO
1805 N. 30th Street (at Gateway Road)
Colorado Springs, CO 80904

WHEN TO GO
Self Guided
Daily
9 am – 5pm

DEGREE OF DIFFICULTY
Easy

CONTACT
719.634.6666
www.gardenofgods.com

IL VICINO

As you enter Il Vicino, located in downtown Colorado Springs, the smell of delicious wood pizza will consume you. The wood oven, in which the pizza is cooked, is located on the far side of the bar. The beer complements the pizza, as both are outstanding in quality.

The hardwood floors lead the way back to the brew tanks used in the process. Encased in the glass wall, the upstairs facility produces delightful brews loved all over Colorado Springs. The remainder of the brewery equipment is downstairs, but you'll need a tour guide to see this area.

The restaurant provides a choice of delicious Italian fare and there's no doubt that half of Colorado Springs knows this place is special! The restaurant decor inspires an image of Italy and clearly exposes the roots of the restaurant. A few of the brews created at Il Vicino are non-alcoholic, and the Da Vinci Root Beer is available for the younger generations.

LOCAL'S CHOICE: Fatty Rice Light Irish Ale, which is barely sweet with a medium body and slight hop bitterness.

TAKE THE TOUR

WHERE TO GO
11 S. Tejon St.
Colorado Springs, CO
80903

WHEN TO GO
Self-Guided
Monday – Thursday
11 –11
Friday – Saturday
11am – midnight
Best times to tour:
2 – 4pm

DEGREE OF DIFFICULTY
Easy

CONTACT
719.475.9224
www.ilvicino.com

JOSH AND JOHN'S ICE CREAM

The owners of Josh and John's Ice Cream are high school buddies, Josh Paris and John Krakauer. After graduating from school, they found themselves in business together, opening one of Colorado's finest ice cream shops.

Learning about the ice cream-making process is the highlight of the tour. In the front section of the store you will see three barrel-like mechanical churns whose arms rotate continuously to mix the ingredients. On the shelves are the ingredients that vary with the day's mixtures. All of the dairy ingredients are locally made and purchased through the Western Dairy Association.

The decor of Josh and John's Ice Cream shop will make you feel at home, with walls featuring highlights from the ice cream shop's history. There are also plenty of awards given for the ice cream's quality.

The delightful visuals include a cow trashcan and a red snake on the wall, and if that is not enough, check out the cow cooler door.

Of course, this tour isn't complete without checking out the flavors of ice cream available at the shop. I recommend the Colorado Cookies and Cream, which tastes like heaven.

TAKE THE TOUR

WHERE TO GO
111 E. Pikes Peak
Colorado Spring, CO

WHEN TO GO
Guided Tour
Reservations required
11am - 10:30pm

DEGREE OF DIFFICULTY
Easy

CONTACT
719.632.0299

PHANTOM CANYON BREWING CO.

The Phantom Canyon Brewery, located in downtown Colorado Springs, is a favorite place for locals who come here to sip a brew and watch the sun set. The brewery offers five staple beers, along with several alternates to choose from. While touring you'll see the brewery equipment situated behind a glass wall near the back of the restaurant. The restaurant, itself, curves artistically around the brewery, which you'll see from the bar or any table. You can also enjoy a brew in the Billiard Hall or on the patio.

The food here is really good, yet reasonably priced. Choose from simple pub-style food or try one of the Colorado-style specialties. Many of their recipes include their brewed beer, such as the Smoked Gouda, made with their Blonde Ale. Whatever you order, you will not be disappointed in your choice, as the food is excellent!

LOCAL'S CHOICE: Queen's Blonde Ale, which is a light, crisp and has a touch of malt taste made with German hops.

SIMPICH CHARACTER DOLLS

Simpich Character Dolls, first created in 1952, are the brainchildren of Bob and Jan Simpich. The then-newlyweds were on a limited budget and began making the dolls as Christmas gifts. Today collectors adore and order dolls made from the shop on Colorado Avenue.

TAKE THE TOUR

WHERE TO GO
2413 W. Colorado Ave.
Colorado Springs, CO 80904
WHEN TO GO
Self-Guided
Monday – Friday
9am – 5pm
CONTACT
719.636.3272
www.simpich.com

The main tour begins in the back of the room and up the staircase. At the top of the stairs is a hall with thousands of doll parts all lined up and organized by theme, such as "angel parts" and "elf parts". Arms, legs and heads wait here until the doll maker is ready to paint and fit them onto their doll. Through the hall is the sewing room, where seamstresses make mini costumes to fit the character themes.

Next up is the painting room, where monochrome dolls become full of color and personality. Craftspeople, at their stations filled with paints, use small brushes to add expressions and minute details to the dolls' faces and bodies. This part of the tour is so interesting!

The tour goes back downstairs to the quality-control room, where every part of the doll is looked over to make sure it is perfect. Even a minor imperfection wouldn't make it past this point.

The approved dolls are then boxed and moved next door to the shipping room. Depending on the number of orders, you may see several dozen dolls waiting to be shipped. On my tour there were dolls lining the shelves waiting to leave. Just past the shipping room is a case filled of old-fashioned dolls made by the Simpichs, and representing how doll making has changed over the years.

The craftspeople at this tour are eager to help visitors learn about their work, and since you'll be only inches away from them, you can ask questions and get quick, informative responses.

US OLYMPIC VISITOR CENTER

TAKE THE TOUR

WHERE TO GO
1750 E. Boulder
Colorado Springs, CO
80909

WHEN TO GO
Guided Tour
Fall and Winter
Monday – Saturday
9am – 4pm
Sunday 10am – 4pm
Summer
Monday – Saturday
9am – 5pm
Sunday 10am- 5pm

DEGREE OF DIFFICULTY
Easy

CONTACT
719.866.4618
www.usolympicteam.org

The US Air Force donated this property, previously the ENT Air Force Base, to the Olympic Committee in 1977. This acquisition was one of the deciding factors in bringing the Olympics to Colorado. The Olympic Visitor Center, open to the public, offers a tour that gives visitors an opportunity to learn about the US Olympic Training Center.

Before entering the US Olympic Visitor Center, you will have the opportunity to take a few photos of the Olympic symbol as well as the digital clock that counts down the number of days until the next Olympics. The tour begins inside the building, where you'll see photographs of the Olympic athletes. The tour guide will take you inside the 225-seat auditorium to watch an informative video that explains what goes on at the facility. The group will then proceed down the Irwin Belk Olympic Path, which will take you closer to the areas where the athletes work and live. The Olympic Path features an interesting collaboration of artwork that represents all the Olympics and Pan American Games.

The pathway leads to the Sports Center I and II buildings, which are the training facilities. The Sports Center I building is a 59,000-square-foot multi-sport gymnasium. Inside is the special swimming flume, which is used to train and test the athletes. This flume features a hyperbaric chamber that can help athletes adjust to various altitudes. The Sports Center II building is a 54,000-square-foot training

facility, with two levels filled with equipment that accommodates nine different sports.

The tour proceeds to the Olympic shooting center, the largest shooting facility in the Western Hemisphere and the third largest in the world. The guide will also lead you through several viewing areas, and you will get to see the gym where athletes work one-on-one with trainers to increase their muscle tone and flexibility. Upstairs there is an awesome view of the Aquatics Center, whose Olympic-size pool contains 810,000 gallons of exactly 81-degree water. There are cameras placed at 12 different angles, so athletes and trainers can monitor workouts. The Athlete Center is not open to the public, but the structure is definitely something to see! This three-story residence hall is where athletes from all over America find their home away from home.

After the tour, the guide will lead you back to the Visitor Center, where you will have the opportunity to view the US Olympic Hall of Fame and Olympic memorabilia displays. There are also several interactive kiosks where you can learn about your favorite Olympic athletes. The US Olympic Spirit Store is located in the center, as well. There are several Olympic items for sale that are exclusive to the store, and the proceeds fund the athletes who are working in the complex. You can also visit the rooftop terrace, where an Olympic flame is on display. This area offers panoramic views of the entire complex and the nearby sports sculpture garden.

UNITED STATES AIR FORCE ACADEMY

TAKE THE TOUR

WHERE TO GO
Visitor's Center
2346 Academy Dr.
Colorado Springs, CO
80840

WHEN TO GO
Self Guided Tour
Monday – Saturday
9am – 6pm

DEGREE OF DIFFICULTY
Easy

CONTACT
719.333.2025
www.usafa.af.mi

The US Air Force Academy offers an excellent opportunity to tour their facility, where you will have the chance to learn why this institution is different, in comparison to other universities. The beautiful scenery that surrounds the Academy includes trails that are open to the public, and inside the buildings there are many exhibits about the Air Force and the university.

The Academy is an active military training facility, with public areas and areas that are clearly marked as off limits. The visitor center is located along the south side of the road, and before entering the building you will have a chance to view a retired B-52 bomber. The Air Force considered this type of fighter plane the backbone of America's manned bomber force for 25 years.

The visitor center is open daily from 9 to 5 and is the ideal place to begin a self-guided tour. Inside are free maps, informational brochures including driving instructions and information about special programs for the public. There are also numerous exhibits inside, including information about the cadets and their lifestyle at the Academy. You will have the chance to learn about the classes and physical education requirements that are necessary to graduate. You'll see how physically

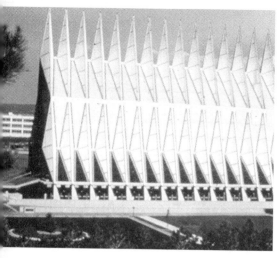

and mentally challenging it is to be a cadet. In the center of the exhibit hall is a large three-dimensional map of the campus. There is also a gift shop, with merchandise displaying the Air Force logo.

One of the Academy's most popular attractions is the Cadet Chapel, accessed by following a trail outside the visitor center. The chapel is considered one of the most distinctive buildings in the country. Another great area to include on your tour is the Thunderbird Airmanship Overlook, where you will have a terrific view of US Air Force A10 Fighter Plane, as well as a chance to see the various flying activities. You will also have the opportunity to tour the Falcon Stadium, where the home football games are played. This is also the location of the famous cadet hat-throwing tradition at graduations.

A tour of US Air Force Academy will give you a new understanding to the lives and accomplishments of the young men and women who attend the university.

VAN BRIGGLE POTTERY

In 1899, the acclaimed potter and sculptor, Artus Van Briggle, with his wife Anne, founded a pottery factory in Colorado Springs. It is the oldest and one of the most respected art facilities still active in the country. Artus studied at the Beaux Arts Academy in Paris and at Rockwood Pottery in Cincinnati, Ohio.

Artus and Anne used clay as a form of poetic expression, carefully patterned pieces with flowing organic lines and simple forms with quiet floral motifs. Each piece is an expression of nature, the human mind and the creative spirit. Often, a piece will exhibit a mixture of all three elements. Using limited color, Artus also reproduced the mat glazes that originated in ancient China.

Pottery-making is considered one of civilization's most ancient art forms and this tour highlights techniques that have been passed down from generation to generation. Upon entering the showroom you will see why the Van Briggle Pottery

TAKE THE TOUR

WHERE TO GO
600 S. 21st St.
Colorado Springs, CO 80904
WHEN TO GO
Self-Guided Tour
Tuesday – Saturday
8:30am – 4:30pm
DEGREE OF DIFFICULTY
Easy
CONTACT
800.847.6341
www.vanbriggle.com

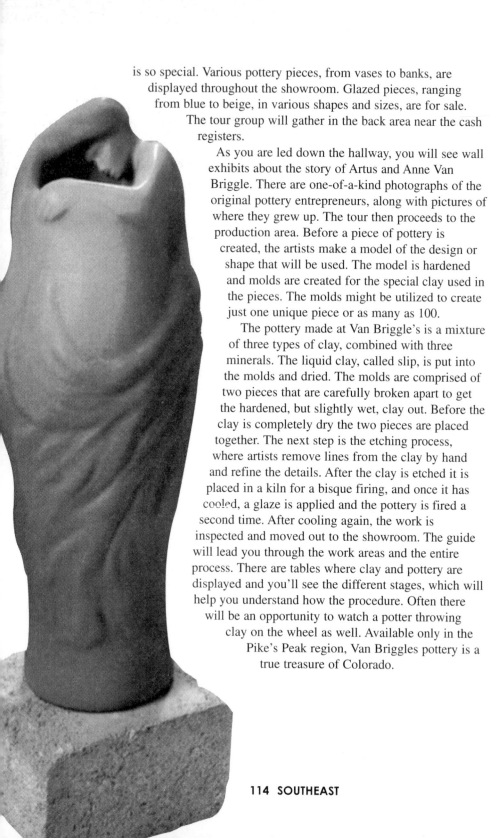

is so special. Various pottery pieces, from vases to banks, are displayed throughout the showroom. Glazed pieces, ranging from blue to beige, in various shapes and sizes, are for sale. The tour group will gather in the back area near the cash registers.

As you are led down the hallway, you will see wall exhibits about the story of Artus and Anne Van Briggle. There are one-of-a-kind photographs of the original pottery entrepreneurs, along with pictures of where they grew up. The tour then proceeds to the production area. Before a piece of pottery is created, the artists make a model of the design or shape that will be used. The model is hardened and molds are created for the special clay used in the pieces. The molds might be utilized to create just one unique piece or as many as 100.

The pottery made at Van Briggle's is a mixture of three types of clay, combined with three minerals. The liquid clay, called slip, is put into the molds and dried. The molds are comprised of two pieces that are carefully broken apart to get the hardened, but slightly wet, clay out. Before the clay is completely dry the two pieces are placed together. The next step is the etching process, where artists remove lines from the clay by hand and refine the details. After the clay is etched it is placed in a kiln for a bisque firing, and once it has cooled, a glaze is applied and the pottery is fired a second time. After cooling again, the work is inspected and moved out to the showroom. The guide will lead you through the work areas and the entire process. There are tables where clay and pottery are displayed and you'll see the different stages, which will help you understand how the procedure. Often there will be an opportunity to watch a potter throwing clay on the wheel as well. Available only in the Pike's Peak region, Van Briggles pottery is a true treasure of Colorado.

GREENWAY & NATURE CENTER OF PUEBLO

The Arkansas River is one of Southern Colorado's greatest secrets. Its headwaters are in the mountains near Leadville, and the flow goes through Canon City, Pueblo and on to Wichita, Kansas. The tour covers both conservation and beauty, but as with any conversation about water rights, there aren't enough solid solutions for difficult problems.

The tour begins in the Information Center, which is located in the gift store. Inside the center are displays

TAKE THE TOUR

WHERE TO GO
Nature Center Road
Pueblo, CO

WHEN TO GO
Self-Guided
Tuesday – Saturday
9am – 5pm

DEGREE OF DIFFICULTY
Easy

CONTACT
719.549.2414
www.csm.uscolo.edu/gnc

about the river and the people who depend on it. Kiosks filled with information describe how we all take water for granted, and how conservation is so important to our water supply. Hopefully, these messages will give kids a lot to think about.

Next up is a chance to see the river, which runs along the boardwalk. Cross the parking lot for the paved path that you can walk on while looking at different segments of the water. You'll learn about the fish that live here, the raptors that inhabit the area, and other facts about the river's importance.

If you are looking to spend a couple of hours, consider stopping at the café along the boardwalk or, better yet, pack a picnic. Listening to the birds sing and watching the water go by makes for a relaxing afternoon.

IRISH BREW PUB AND GRILLE

TAKE THE TOUR

WHERE TO GO
108 W. Third St.
Pueblo, CO 81002

WHEN TO GO
Guided Tour
Monday – Friday
1 - 4pm
Reservations required

DEGREE OF DIFFICULTY
Easy

CONTACT
719 542.9974
www.pueblonline.com/irishpub

The Irish Brew Pub and Grille has been a family-owned business since 1944, but the brewery has only been around since 1996, creating special beers for the Southern Colorado area. One thing you will notice upon entering the brewery is the unique bar. Spanning more than 20 feet, the dark wood-stained centerpiece looks like it's from a Wild West movie.

The food featured on the menu is quite extraordinary: If lobster or shrimp are not your desire, you might consider the outback ostrich burgers with salad. The pasta combinations are elaborate, and there are special dishes prepared for vegetarians.

The brewery equipment takes up about a quarter of the restaurant space and it can be seen from windows facing the street. One of the specialties from the brewery is the exotic Chili Beer, in which Mexican-roasted Pueblo chili extract is used! Additionally, the pub is known for featuring special seasonal and holiday brews, such as the strong red ale available around St. Patrick's Day.

LOCAL'S CHOICE: Steel City Lager, which follows a traditional lager brewing process with cold aging, to reveal a clear, crisp flavor.

BISHOP CASTLE

You could call Bishop Castle a works-in-progress. Since 1969, Jim Bishop has been constructing his dream: a castle within the forest. Now, you may think castles are only found in Europe, but this one sits only four hours from the Denver-metro area. The creator wants to share his dream with others, so he allows the public to explore the castle and its surrounding trails.

In 1959, when he was 15, Mr. Bishop paid 200 bucks for the 2-acre property that's surrounded on three sides San Isabel National Forest. Originally, his idea was to build a summer cottage on the lot, but Bishop couldn't get water to the site. Then he placed a 4,000-gallon cistern on the land, and surrounded it with a stone wall. After that first addition, the cottage began to grow. Over the first eight years, friends offered to help build the cottage, but no one actually assisted – not even one person.

Jim will tell you that building a castle is labor-intensive. He's handled each stone an average of six times. What's made it especially difficult is that the mortar used to set the rocks in place is temperature-sensitive, making for a short construction season in Colorado. The highest point of the castle is the 30-foot-tall steel steeple atop the masonry, making it about 160 feet, or 16 floors high.

While adults appreciate the castle's architecture, kids love the dragon. In the mid 1980s a truckload of stainless steel warming plates was unloaded at Jim's iron shop, in Pueblo. Throughout the winter, Jim hammered the steel into scales that would be placed on the giant dragon that, today, sits perched off the Grand Ballroom, 80 feet in the air. Later came a hot air balloon burner, turning this into a fire-breathing dragon when ignited, in summer.

Your castle tour can be as long or short as you like. During daylight hours, you can see how one man built an architectural wonder that defies all the schooled thoughts of building. Since the castle is far up in the mountains, you may want to consider bringing a picnic to enjoy the sites, hike around the castle and relax.

The Bishop family doesn't own the castle anymore. They donated it to a non-profit organization so the public can enjoy the free castle in Colorado and the Rocky Mountain Region.

TAKE THE TOUR

WHERE TO GO
San Isabel National Forest, CO
WHEN TO GO
Self Guided
Daily: Dusk to Dawn
CONTACT
719.485.3040
www.bishopcastle.org

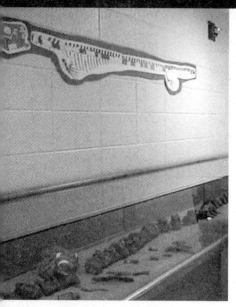

LOUDEN-HENRITZE ARCHAEOLOGY MUSEUM

On the lower level of the Samuel Freudenthal Memorial Library, on the Trinidad State College campus, you will find a little-known treasure: an archaeological museum. The Trinidad State Junior College Archaeology Department was established in 1942 under the direction of Norman Dondelinger and Robert Tatum. The role of the museum is to help preserve and educate interests found in historical and archaeological sites throughout Las Animas County.

Many of the artifacts on display were from digs sponsored by the college. Among the most interesting are the mammoth tusk and bones recovered near Kim, in 1966. Another interesting specimen is a fossilized skeleton of a prehistoric reptile, unearthed near the Trinidad Power Plant. Looking back to Colorado's prehistoric times gives us an opportunity to understand how fragile our environment is today.

The rock shelter, a replica of the Trinchera Shelter, is one place you'll want to spend a little extra time. By studying the shelter and its contents, scientists have gained information about cultures that had inhabited this area about 1,000 years ago. Now one should be wondering how perishable items and material possessions could last that long. Because of the cave's location, it was protected from harsh weather conditions and stayed dry inside. The items found at this shelter include braided ropes, grass mats, yucca sandals and more. One of the more current finds highlighted in the museum is the fossilized remains of a Mosasaur, discovered during construction of a home in Trinidad. The partial skeleton is a 32- 36-foot-long tylosaurus.

While adults will marvel at the artifacts, replicas of the fossilized dinosaur prints will excite the kids. One of the prints is from a Tyrannosaurus Rex, the other a duck-bill dinosaur. All are from the Las Animas County area.

TAKE THE TOUR

WHERE TO GO
Samuel Freudenthal
Memorial Library
Ground Floor
Trinidad State Junior College
Trinidad, CO 81082

WHEN TO GO
Self Guided Tour
January – November
Monday – Friday
10am – 4pm

DEGREE OF DIFFICULTY
Easy

CONTACT
719.846.5508
www.trinidadstate.edu
/museum

COLORADO

DURANGO

PAGOSA SPRINGS

SALIDA

SOUTHWEST

DURANGO FISH HATCHERY

One of the oldest fish hatcheries in Colorado is located in Durango. The first hatchery building was constructed in 1893 to facilitate the fish-stocking programs, which began in the early 1900s. With the abundance of fishermen, the state realized it was necessary to stock the waters in order to save fish from extinction. The hatcheries in the western part of the state are involved with cold-water fish such as Native Cutthroat, Kokanee and Rainbow Trout.

Today the Durango State Trout Hatchery and Rearing Unit is a composition of raceways, nurse ponds and a show pond. The hatchery stocks 56 streams and 65 lakes and reservoirs, located mostly in the Animas River drainage. This is the perfect tour for families, so bring the kids and plenty of film.

The hatchery is divided into two parts, and the first side deals exclusively with rainbow trout. These fish are not native to Colorado, but they were imported into the state in 1882 from California. They are a popular catch in the Rocky Mountain region, especially for those who enjoy fishing as a pastime.

The other side of the hatchery is used for breeding other types of trout. Native Cutthroat Trout are artificially spawned on location, and Kokanee and Kokanee Salmon eggs are obtained each fall from the nearby Dolores River. The Rainbow

TAKE THE TOUR
WHERE TO GO
151 E. 16th Street
Durango, CO 81301
WHEN TO GO
Self-Guided Tour
Visitor Center and
Wildlife Museum
May – Labor Day
Call for Hours
Guided Tour for School
Groups
DEGREE OF DIFFICULTY
Easy
CONTACT
970.259.0501

Fish eggs are brought in from outside sources and raised to the proper sizes. This becomes a massive project, as 1.5 million fish, which are grown from egg to a catchable size, move through this part of the hatchery annually.

Inside the hatchery you will see the fish swimming around in raceways, which are long concrete pools that allow the fish to swim back and forth while growing to the appropriate size. A show pond in front of the hatchery provides a look at other fish found on the premises.

Another interesting section of the hatchery is the nurse ponds. These are smaller pools for the fish that are in the fingerling stage. They are kept here until they grow to about two to five inches. You will have the chance to see a number of fish in this area, especially if you tour during the feeding times. There is another hatchery building that is for the smallest fish, from egg to two inches long.

If you enjoy fish, check out the nifty little machines located near the raceways. For two bits you can buy food from the machine and feed the fish. Usually the fish come to the top of the raceway and quickly gulp down the food.

You may wonder how fish find their way to the lakes and streams around Colorado. According to the hatchery, airplanes and helicopters plant the one- to two-inch fish, and they backpack or horseback ride the one- to four-inch fish to more appropriate, hard-to-reach places. The two- to four-inch fish and the larger nine- to ten-inch fish ready to catch are moved by tank truck. Pretty amazing!

The hatchery is located next to the Animas River and you can conclude the tour by taking a walk downstream to catch a glimpse of the spectacular views!

FACT: 140,000 pounds of feed are used for 1 million fish

ECHO MOUNTAIN ALPACAS

You might think that you've seen a dragon when you pull into the driveway of the Echo Mountain Alpacas Ranch. The creatures here are rarely seen anywhere else, let alone the local zoo. Alpacas are from the camel family, and they are raised exclusively for their soft coat. These animals grow a fiber which is similar to silk. It's hypoallergenic and is a commodity among cottage spinners and weavers worldwide.

The tour of the facility takes a couple of hours, but it's well worth the time. The opportunity to see these soft, yet tall creatures in their own environment will give you a different perspective about an animal that is not even remotely native to Colorado. After looking at an alpaca you might get the impression that they really love living in the area and enjoy the clean mountain air.

The tour begins with a presentation on the alpacas, and you will learn more in-depth information about their origins and why they are here in Colorado. The guide will also give an overview about the food they eat and the special conditions of the ranch. They will also take the time to show you how the animals are exercised and explain the type of care the animals require. The area surrounding the ranch is beautiful! In the San Juan Mountains of southwestern Colorado, you might want to be an alpaca just to live on this great ranch.

The second half of the presentation includes information about the alpaca's fleece. After being removed from the animal, it is woven into finished products. The fleece is placed on a spinning wheel, and there will be a demonstration of the weaving loom process. This part of the tour is especially great for the kids, as they will have the opportunity to learn how clothing items were made about fifty to one hundred years ago. The ranch sells items which are made from the fleece, including sweaters, scarves and hats.

Owned by Dave and Suzy Belt, the ranch is known worldwide for its participation in the alpaca industry. The Belts are active in the community, and they take the animals around for all to see. They also publish *Alpacas Magazine*, which is an international magazine dedicated to raising these animals.

TAKE THE TOUR

TAKE THE TOUR
Where to go
678 Dichoso Street
Pagosa Springs, CO 81147

WHEN TO GO
Guided Tour
Tuesday and Thursday
1pm
Call Ahead

DEGREE OF DIFFICULTY
Moderate

CONTACT
970.731.2729

MOUNTAIN SPIRIT WINERY

TAKE THE TOUR

WHERE TO GO
15750 County Road 220
Salida, CO 81201

WHEN TO GO
Guided Tour
Monday – Saturday
10am – 5pm

DEGREE OF DIFFICULTY
Easy

CONTACT
719.539.1175
www.mountainspiritwinery.com

In the Arkansas River Valley, about 12 miles west of Salida, you will find one of the best wineries in the Rocky Mountain region. Mountain Spirit Winery is situated on five acres of farmland, which is surrounded by 14,000-foot mountain vistas, and apple orchards in the area near an old homestead house. The views in the summertime are absolutely breathtaking, and a stop here will provide relaxation for those looking to get away from the daily grind of city life.

The owners, Terry and Michael Barkett, are winemakers who continue to push the limits of exploring new blends, while maintaining the traditional historic standards inherent in the art of winemaking. Specializing in creating unique blends of wine using fruit and grapes, the winery has won awards every year of their existence. The opportunities to taste the wine are found at the winery as well as at the nifty little store in Salida.

One of the wines that find plenty of customers is the blend of unexposed merlot and raspberry wine. It is unrefined but sterile filtered to give delightful fruity flavors with a crisp clean taste. This wonderful spirit is an excellent accompaniment to beef and lamb.

COLORADO

ASPEN

BRECKENRIDGE

ESTES PARK

GLENWOOD
SPRINGS

GRAND
JUNCTION

IDAHO SPRINGS

PALISADE

VAIL

NORTHWEST

ASPEN DOWNTOWN WALKING TOUR

Heritage Aspen, Aspen's Historical Society, has put together an exciting self-guided walking tour of downtown. Take a couple of hours to study the architecture and to enjoy the relaxing atmosphere and Aspen's friendly folks.

The tour starts at the Wheeler Opera House, the best place to pick up the free map offered by the Historical Society. In 1889, its construction costs reached $80,000, a pricey ticket at the time, but one that also earned the Opera House the reputation of being one of the best such venues in the state. Then the house hit unpredictable times: Because of extensive fire damage, the upper floors were closed until its restoration in 1956. There were other problems over the years, as well, including lack of community support and financial concerns. Then, in 1984, the City of Aspen took ownership and permanently reopened the Wheeler Opera House.

The next stop on the tour is the Mother Lode, one of the few authentic, false-front buildings remaining in the area. Much like the old ghost-town buildings you'd see in western movies, false-fronts give the impression that the building is taller than one story. Just down the street is the Crystal Palace, the next stop on the tour. Opened in 1891 as a wholesale house, this building has experienced several personality changes and changes in ownership. Finally, in the 1960s it became a restaurant and popular venue for musical reviews. Next up is the the Aspen Times Building, housing the local rag since 1905. The Times, however, predates the building, as B. Clark Wheeler purchased the paper in 1885, when he decided to make it a daily. It is Aspen's oldest continuously published newspaper.

TAKE THE TOUR
WHERE TO GO
320 E. Hyman Street
Aspen, CO 81611
WHEN TO GO
Self-Guided Tour
Daily
Map at the Wheeler Opera House Visitor's Center
DEGREE OF DIFFICULTY
Moderate
CONTACT
970.920.5770

The tour continues as you walk along the historical streets of the city. Make sure you take time to stop at the Old Fire Bell. Henry Gillespie gave this silver bell to the city in 1886, when the 2,300-pound icon was carried over the mountains by mule train. Hauling it up steep mountain inclines with animals was slow and

arduous, taking months before finally arriving.

The tour ends at the Lift 1 Site. Lift 1, opened by the Aspen Skiing Company in 1947, was the longest chairlift in the world, at the time. It was abandoned in 1971, when a two-person chair was installed. Today the site is reserved for a future museum.

HOLDEN/MAROLT MINING & RANCHING MUSEUM

The town of Aspen was originally founded as a silver mining camp. In 1890, Aspen was the largest producer of silver in America and, with 13,000 people, it was the third-largest city in Colorado. Thousands came to Aspen looking for wealth, but it wasn't to be found.

At the edge of Aspen is the 22-acre Holden Lixiviation Mill. Using a process to refine low-grade ore, the plant pulled $68,000 worth of silver out of the mountains before going broke 14 months later. The process involved crushing, heating and salting techniques to refine as little as ten ounces of silver from one ton of ore. Five- to six-thousand tons of salt was shipped monthly from Salt Lake City for the process. At the time, the average take was 400 – 600 ounces of silver per ton, but the lower grade of ore had no chance of producing such amounts of refined silver. When the furnaces were heating full-throttle, smoke from the mill could be seen throughout the valley. The smoke stacks at the plant were 165 feet high – said to be the tallest of the land.

Your tour gives you a first-hand look at the mill. Hiking trails, established by the City of Aspen, are a short walk away, and it's on this land that ore was shoveled off the carts. The building you'll see is the Sampling Mill. In 1940 the Marolt family bought the entire mill for only a dollar, and combined it with their ranch to raise sheep and cattle and to farm potatoes.

Today, equipment is littered along the front lawn of the building. From ore carts to tractor parts, you'll see some of the machinery used to cultivate the land. The informational signs next to the walkway are worth reading. Old-time photographs show how miners where checked to assure consistency in the quality of their ore shipment. There's also information about ranching in the Aspen area.

Currently, you cannot wander inside the buildings unless someone is around.

TAKE THE TOUR
WHERE TO GO
7th Street and Main
Aspen, CO 81611
WHEN TO GO
Self-Guided Tour
Daily: Dusk – Dawn
DEGREE OF DIFFICULTY
Easy
CONTACT
970.925.3721

TAKE THE TOUR

WHERE TO GO
600 S. Main Street
Breckenridge, CO 80424

WHEN TO GO
Guided & Self-Guided Tours
Daily 11am – 2am
Reservations Required for Guided Tour

DEGREE OF DIFFICULTY
Easy

CONTACT
970.453.1550
www.breckbrew.com

BRECKENRIDGE BREWERY

Breckenridge Brewery is the perfect location for the tired skier who needs a brew to reflect on the fun. Since it is known for its great beers, plenty of the locals and many of the ski buffs and other visitors enjoy an afternoon at this brewery. Being the only brewery in Breckenridge, it's a hit with the community. After it was founded in 1990, a demand quickly grew to include liquor stores in Vail and Aspen. Today there are two additional breweries in Denver and one in Buffalo, New York.

The layout of the brewery is unique. As you would assume, the brewery equipment is easy to spot. However, if you are looking for the perfect place to sit,

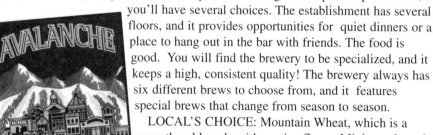

you'll have several choices. The establishment has several floors, and it provides opportunities for quiet dinners or a place to hang out in the bar with friends. The food is good. You will find the brewery to be specialized, and it keeps a high, consistent quality! The brewery always has six different brews to choose from, and it features special brews that change from season to season.

LOCAL'S CHOICE: Mountain Wheat, which is a smooth golden ale with a spicy flavor. Mixing pale and wheat malts and the combination of Washington Hallertau and Czechoslovakian Saaz hops gives a unique flavor to the ale.

BRECKENRIDGE DOWNTOWN HISTORICAL TOUR NORTH MAIN

Breckenridge's history has long been oriented around mining and skiing. A walking tour, divided into two sections, was developed in the late 1990s to give visitors a glimpse of Colorado's rich past. Highlights of the tour include taking steps back in time, to learn about the places and people who made this area rich in culture and personality. The Main Street Tour in Breckenridge is divided into two sections: North and South Main. This part of the tour is North Main.

Historically, 324 North Main marked the northern boundary. The teamster, Albert Schatz moved ore from the mines to the mills, and coal to local homes and businesses. His workforce included the stock of several teams of mules, horses and a number of wagons and sleds. Before actually moving to Breckenridge, he supplied the mining camps with potatoes from his ranch.

Walking a bit farther, you can check out a Boomtown Cottage, an architectural style borrowed from the East Coast. The cottage, built before 1886, is a simple one-story house with a side entrance.

The Editor's House, situated at 111 North Main, dates to 1880 and was occupied by the John Cooper Fincher family in the early 1900s. Mr. Fincher was the founder of the Breckenridge Daily Journal. He never actually lived in the house as the name

TAKE THE TOUR	
WHERE TO GO	Downtown Breckenridge
WHEN TO GO	Self-Guided Tour Daily Maps available at the Summit Activity Center
DEGREE OF DIFFICULTY	Moderate
CONTACT	970.453.9022

implied, but his family did. The newspaper office is down the street in a building that was once home to the Daily Journal and the Summit County Journal. The classic western false-front building was used by the Journal's printing office until it moved in 1981.

Next door is the Chinese Laundry Building. "Choy Chinaman" and three employees washed and dried clothing here. They pressed the pieces by shoving the iron back and forth while blowing water out of their mouths and onto the clothes. Choy celebrated Chinese New Year by giving out snacks to his customers.

The tour ends near Rankin's Hotel. In the 1860s James Rankin went to Breckenridge with more than just thoughts of gold. He assumed the gold seekers would be tired and hungry once they arrived, and opened the hotel before 1869 in hopes of cashing in on their needs. The friendly inn wasn't the sure bet Rankin thought it would be, but regulars enjoyed the Palace Restaurant and the smoke-filled, whiskey-scented, amusement hall.

On a sunny day, any time of the year, a walking tour of the historic downtown brings to life the daily routines of the miners and pioneers who came here. While you are looking at the buildings, don't forget to look inside at the great stores, too.

BRECKENRIDGE DOWNTOWN
HISTORICAL TOUR SOUTH MAIN

Breckenridge is known for awesome skiing and great summer concerts. Another side of "Breck" is its historical importance. The Breckenridge Downtown Historical Walking Tour is divided into two parts, this one, the South tour, reflects the mining and architectural relevance to the city. Pick up a map at the Summit Activity Center, or the information centers on Main Street.

Continuing south on Main, this portion highlights 28 significant buildings. Roby's Tore, on 101 South Main, is the first stop. In 1866 John Roby opened his general store as an outfitter for those who came in search of gold. They paid a pretty penny, too, being there was no other place for miles where they could purchase supplies. The building is a wood-frame example of the Italianate style.

If you were looking for a hot or cold bath in 1886 you would have headed to Brush's Barbershop and Confectionery, on 115 South Main. Two bits would have bought you a bath, haircut, and bite to eat. Minnie Brush owned the confectionery, a popular place for customers who would come to relax on wire-backed chairs while sipping their choice of drinks at the marble soda fountain.

For a belt, after a long day's work, folks would head to The Miner's Home Saloon. This false-front western-style building was originally lined with barn wood. The Saloon moved into town around 1881 and was the place for miners sharing information about the faro tables.

Farther down the street, stops include the house of Nels Pherson, a talented carpenter by trade, who helped build much of Breckenridge – including this house

> **TAKE THE TOUR**
>
> **WHERE TO GO**
> Downtown Breckenridge
>
> **WHEN TO GO**
> Self-Guided Tour
> Daily
> Maps available at the
> Summit Activity Center
>
> **DEGREE OF DIFFICULTY**
> Moderate
>
> **CONTACT**
> 970.453.9022

where he lived. In 1909, he expanded the house to include the semicircular arches around the windows and the front porch roof. Next door is the C.O. Lindquist House, the largest residence on Main Street.

The tour ends at the Undertakers House, at 300 South Main. Milton Huntress, known as "Deacon," was originally the manager of the Denver Hotel. Stress drove him to change professions, and he turned to furniture-building and undertaking. He, along with Harry Rogers, bought the town's first horse-drawn hearse in 1891.

THE BALDPATE INN

TAKE THE TOUR

WHERE TO GO
4900 S. Highway 7
Estes Park, CO 80517

WHEN TO GO
Self-Guided Tour
May – October
Daily 9 – 9

DEGREE OF DIFFICULTY
Easy

CONTACT
970.586.6151
www.baldpateinn.com

If you have ever lost your house or car keys, they just may be waiting for you at the Baldpate Inn. Here you can find a set of keys to open just about everything. Over 20,000 keys line the ceiling, walls and beams.

According to Lois Smith, proprietor of The Baldpate Inn, there are keys to about everything. Why keys? The original owners Gordon and Ethel Mace built the inn in 1917, and named it after the mystery novel *Seven Keys to Baldpate*, by Earl Derr Biggers. The author had visited the property and noted how similar it was to his imaginary Baldpate Inn. In the novel, seven visitors traveled to the hotel, each thinking that he or she held the only key. Keeping with the tradition of the story, the Mace family would give each visitor a key to keep. But during World War I, metal became too expensive and the Maces asked guests instead, to bring them a key. Hence, a tradition began.

Some of the examples you'll see here are not ordinary keys. The first United Airlines Mainliner, from California to New York, stopped through Denver on May 15, 1937. The key used, along with an explanation, hangs from the wall. Deck keys from cruise liners and the key to the first 12-car Denver *Zephyr* train are here, too. Ok – so you can't think of any other kinds of keys? How about briefcase keys, a hut key from Korea, a hubcap key, a thermometer key, the key to the El Paso Texas Library, the key to a roll-top desk, the key to the Denver Theater, and the key from the Frankenstein Castle in Breman, Germany. Still not impressed? Then come check out keys to Buckingham Palace, the Vatican, the Denver County Jail, and how about a key to nothing!

The keys are tagged and systematically organized, although many do look the same. On the beams are keys from various states; on the crossbeam are keys from

Colorado; special keys are in cases; and oversize keys are on the benches.

When you've had your fill here, remember to donate one of your own keys. Giving up a key has become such a popular tradition that Baldpate receives keys in the mail regularly.

The other interest here is photography. Charles and Stuart Mace, brothers of the original owners, were both professional photographers. In 1911 Charles Mace, who was General John J. Pershing's personal photographer, was awarded first prize in an Eastman Kodak national photo contest. After he returned from the war, he worked as a photojournalist in Denver. He captured legends such as Henry Ford, Thomas Edison, Theodore Roosevelt and Buffalo Bill, in a style rarely seen in photographs from that era.

ESTES PARK BREWERY

If you like beer and chili along with the beauty of Longs Peak, the Estes Park Brewery is the place for you. The brewery and restaurant are located in a two-story building, and you can stop by for dinner or a free brew sample. Downstairs you will see the open counter where you can try a sample. There are plenty of refrigerators with fresh brew ready to take home, and their logo merchandise can be purchased downstairs as well.

Upstairs is the nostalgic dining area with a small bar. Presented in a rustic cabin approach, the room makes you feel as though you have walked miles to the nearest trading post and are among friends. The restaurant offers All-American fare with a few unique qualities. The homemade beer chili is what the locals swear by, and I suggest you try some if you'd like a taste of great Colorado chili. It's made with Trail Ridge Red Beer, and the chili can be eaten alone or with hamburgers, hot dogs or buffalo burgers. No matter how it's served, you'll be tasting something great.

The brewery, which can be viewed from the second floor, provides ten handcrafted beers on tap with three of them being seasonal. From the window on the second floor, you can see the whole brewery operation, from the grain storage to the fermentation tanks. I suspect after the tour you will direct your attention to the west windows and the gorgeous view of the mountains. the Estes Park Brewery is a perfect place for a brew with a view.

LOCAL'S CHOICE: The Trail Ridge Red, which is a smooth deep-colored red ale made with American hops and English malts.

TAKE THE TOUR

WHERE TO GO
470 Prospect Village Drive
Estes Park, CO 80517

WHEN TO GO
Self-Guided Tour
Monday – Thursday
11am – 8pm
Friday – Saturday
11am – 8pm

DEGREE OF DIFFICULTY
Easy

CONTACT
970.586.5421
www.epbrewery.com

MICHAEL RICKER PEWTER

Michael Anthony Ricker is considered to be one of the most talented pewter artists in the world. His main gallery is located in Estes Park Valley, and this is where the pewter molding is done. There are 12 Michael Ricker galleries throughout the United States, and if you are interested in American culture and art, a tour of the museum will give you a glimpse into the ingenious mind of a famous sculptor!

Michael Ricker is a very talented person, and his gift shop is overflowing with beautiful pieces, which many collectors review and purchase. His images capture everything from mythology to sports figures. Mr. Ricker has been an artist for over 40 years, and he has worked in pewter materials for 35 years.

An interesting aspect of Mr. Ricker's career is how he became an international artist. In 1985, he presented a piece titled *Park City – America Remembered*, to former President Gerald Ford. The piece is not a small work; it spans an entire wall and it required a total of $700,000 to complete. Highlighting professions and issues in America, the artist created an amazing piece, which includes individual people and their surroundings, which he presented in a realistic atmosphere. The Smithsonian Institution owns the piece, and they have been kind enough to allow the gallery to display it.

The tour guide will take you through the gallery, and you will also be able to review letters which congratulate Michael Ricker and provide encouragement. You will also get to see photographs of the artist with famous celebrities.

TAKE THE TOUR

WHERE TO GO
2050 Big Thompson Ave.
Highway 34 East
Estes Park, CO 80517

WHEN TO GO
Guided Tour
Monday – Friday
9am – 5pm
Sunday
11am – 5pm

DEGREE OF DIFFICULTY
Easy

CONTACT
970.586.2030
800.373.9837
www.ricker.com

The pewter pieces and die casts exhibited in the gallery will not be found in the gift shop, as most of the works are exclusive series. You will have the opportunity to view hundreds of works that are displayed in themes, and there are also works that were commissioned by the Olympic Committee and Walt Disney.

Michael Ricker loves rabbits and children. However, all of his pewter pieces are absolutely impressive and worth the view. As a native of Colorado, born and raised in Fort Collins, he has stuck to his roots of the state and his company employs over 100 people.

FACT: Michael Ricker was asked to create a sculpture of the Pope when he visited the United States.

THE STANLEY HOTEL

Most of us know the Stanley Hotel from the film adaptation of Stephen King's horrifying novel, *The Shining.* However, there is much more to this quaint hotel, situated in Estes Park. A tour of the commanding white building with red roof may be just what the doctor ordered.

F.O. Stanley was diagnosed with tuberculosis and sent to Colorado from Massachusetts, to relieve the suffering. Soon after he and his wife arrived in Denver in 1903, his symptoms began to improve, so they continued on to Estes Park. In the Estes Valley, he continued to recover and both of them fell in love with the Rocky Mountains.

Construction on the Stanley Hotel began in 1906, and Stanley and architect Robert Weiger supervised the work as the buildings took shape. Stanley chose the neoclassical Georgian-Colonial Revival style, with columns and pilasters that made the building stand out.

The hotel, which was electrified, opened in 1909, and a hydroelectric plant was built to provide power to the hotel and the entire Estes Village. Every room had running water, indoor facilities, a tub and a telephone. This was an amazing feat, as even people who lived on the Front Range didn't have these luxuries. News of the resort spread, word of mouth, bringing many customers to the valley. Some came up for the weekend, others for weeks at a time.

Today's hotel management allows guests to wander the main floors of the hotel. There's a grand lobby, culminating in the MacGregor Room. The Music Room and the Pinon Room are large in style and decor, as they reflect the beauty of the turn of the 20th century.

Downstairs, the museum is open to the public. Interesting little facts about the Stanleys make the visit even more enjoyable. The original name of the hotel was not going to be Stanley, but Dunraven, after the man who previously owned the land. Another interesting fact is how guests got to the hotel. It was the first resort to use the Stanley Steamer Mountain Wagon to pick up guests at train station. In the museum you will also see a Stanley violin, made by F.O. Stanley and his brother. What was a hobby, turned into a business in 1924; after F.O.'s death and until 1954, his nephew ran the company and built the instruments.

You'll see pictures of the Stanley family and of the Estes area lining the walls in the museum. Snapshots that are more recent are displayed inside frames and featuring famous people who have been guests at the Stanley including, of course, Stephen King.

GLENWOOD CANYON BREWING COMPANY

The Denver Hotel can be seen from the I-70 highway when you are driving through the Glenwood Springs area. The hotel has a grand piano in the lobby, and it is considered a historical site. It was built on the site of a liquor bottling company that was in operation from 1906-1920, so you are in good company!

Plenty of locals gather at this unique brewery, which is located across the street from the Amtrak station and near the hot springs. The bar and restaurant might make you feel as though you are in a rustic mountain mining hall, and the brewery has a charming atmosphere which relates to the heritage of the West.

You will find six regular brews and two seasonal brews at the Glenwood Canyon Brewing Company, and the brewing equipment can be seen from the front foyer or while sitting at the bar. All of the beers are unpasteurized and they are served at cellar temperature.

LOCAL'S CHOICE: Hanging Lake Honey Ale, which is a light ale with local honey to add extra taste.

TAKE THE TOUR

WHERE TO GO
Hotel Denver
402 Seventh Street
Glenwood Springs, CO
81601

WHEN TO GO
Self-Guided Tour
Daily
11am – Noon
Reservations Required for Guided Tour

DEGREE OF DIFFICULTY
Easy

CONTACT
970.945.1276

**www.thehoteldenver.com
/brewpub**

ENSTROM'S CANDIES

TAKE THE TOUR

WHERE TO GO
200 S. 7th Street
Grand Junction, CO 81502

WHEN TO GO
Guided Tour
Monday – Friday
8:30am – 5pm
Saturday
9am – 5pm
Reservations Required

DEGREE OF DIFFICULTY
Easy

CONTACT
800.367.8766
800.ENSTROM
www.enstrom.com

When you walk into the headquarters of Enstrom's in Grand Junction, the smell of candy will overwhelm you! Enstrom's was founded in 1960, by Chet and Vernie Enstrom, and they are a third generation small business.

They began as a small mom and pop operation making candy, almost exclusively focusing on Chet's special recipe almond toffee. As the toffee's reputation developed in Colorado, the sweet delight took a life of its own and orders grew to 10,000 pounds in 1965. That same year they sold the business to their son Emil and his wife Mary. They continued with the almond toffee production, reaching 150,000 pounds in 1979 and catering to a national market. The third generation of Enstrom, Chet's granddaughter Jamee and her husband Doug Simons, bought the business in 1993. They have brought the production to a half-million pounds of almond toffee annually. The famous toffee is shipped in one-, two-, three- or five-pound boxes around the United States and to locations in fifty foreign countries. They have also have developed an ordering website, which is accessible to everyone.

The view in the lobby will give you an opportunity to learn how they make their famous toffee. Morning's are usually the best time to visit the shop and watch how the toffee is made, and according to the employees before 1pm is best.

The almond toffee batches weigh about 70 pounds each, and a new batch is made in the morning every fifteen to twenty minutes. Around 2,000 pounds of toffee are made every weekday. The first step to perfect toffee is the ingredients. Using fresh dairy products, they cook butter, sugar and almonds in a copper kettle over a large gas stove. With an automatic mixing machine, which is built into the kettle, the ingredients are mixed together until the mixture is just the right temperature for the toffee to be soft and consistent. It requires two people to move the copper kettle to one of the six tables, where the hot mixture is placed in a heap on the table. The hot toffee is flattened on the tabletops, cooled by water running through the top of the table, and pulled apart to make an even surface. Next the confection is covered with milk chocolate and almond morsels. After it is smoothed down with flat metal knives it is allowed to cool. Once it has been cut into slabs and smaller pieces, the toffee is moved to the packing room, where the employees prepare it for immediate shipment to toffee lovers around the world.

The process of making toffee is elaborate at Enstrom's. Twenty pounds of butter is required for every batch of toffee, and it takes up to four people to make it. The copper kettles are lined up in the kitchen, ready for the toffee showdown every morning when the candy craftspeople come to work.

This unique candy producer is one of the few who reside in Colorado, and they welcome all of us for a sample of their delicious almond toffee and a view of their candy production.

TOMMYKNOCKER BREWERY

The Tommyknocker Brewery is located in downtown Idaho Springs, and it's the perfect place to enjoy the beautiful mountain views while sipping a seriously crafted high country brew. The brewery is named after the mythical elves which supposedly live in the mines.

Many of the miners believed that the tommyknockers kept watch over them during times of trouble, and they are considered to be the guardian angels of the mining industry. There are three types of tommyknockers known in the Idaho Springs area, which include the friendly tommyknocker, the mischievous tommyknocker, and finally the tommyknocker who is on the beer bottles from the brewery.

The restaurant features excellent food, and many of the dishes are made with the handcrafted brews. You will be welcome to look over the brewing equipment to learn more about how their special brews are made. The Tommyknocker Brewery has nine brews on tap, with a specialty brew that rotates seasonally.

LOCAL'S CHOICE: The Maple Nut Brown beer combines the taste of malt with maple syrup from Canada, and it has a style of its own.

TAKE THE TOUR

WHERE TO GO
1401 Miner Street
Idaho Springs, CO 80452

WHEN TO GO
Guided Tour
Monday – Friday
1 – 5pm
Reservations Required

DEGREE OF DIFFICULTY
Easy

CONTACT
303.567.2688
www.tommyknocker.com

COTTONWOOD CELLARS

TAKE THE TOUR

WHERE TO GO
5482 Highway 348
Olathe, CO 81425

WHEN TO GO
Guided Tour
Wednesday – Saturday
11am – 6pm

DEGREE OF DIFFICULTY
Easy

CONTACT
970.323.6224
www.cottonwoodcellars.com

It's been said that once you come to Colorado, you'll want to stay! The owners of Cottonwood Cellars, Diana and Keith Read, seem to have followed this prediction. They arrived in Colorado with the intention of retiring after their careers in computer consulting. However, their time here has been anything but restful, since they own one of Colorado's most distinctive wineries.

After working extensively with a local vintner, Keith Read produced his first bottle of spirits in 1994. The early wines were made from grapes purchased elsewhere in Colorado, while they patiently waited for their crops to mature. Over ten acres have come to full maturity, and they are harvested for the Cottonwood wines.

Today Cottonwood Cellars is considered a major player in the wine industry. A tour and tasting at their facility is an exciting opportunity to learn more about the process and sip flavors that tickle the tongue. The Reads have won many awards for their wine, from places such as the Telluride Wine Festival. I predict that they will win many more, as their wines are a sipping pleasure with the simplest of dinners.

CANYON WIND

CANYON WIND CELLARS

Located next to the Colorado River, Canyon Wind Cellars seems to be the perfect spot for winemaking. A long driveway will lead you into a parking lot next to the tasting room, and the crops can be seen in the fields on both sides of your vehicle as you enter.

Once you get past the elaborate grape fields, you'll need to check out the patio in front of the tasting room. It's a nice place to sit for a moment and casually consider the wine tasting ahead. Inside the tasting room, bottles of wine will be available for you to taste, with a red and white variety available.

While you are sampling the delights of the palate in the tasting room, take a look though the window for a view of the storage room, where the wine barrels are kept. You will have a chance to ask the guide questions about the winemaking industry, and this is a great place to start thinking about how wine is actually made. The employees are gracious and knowledgeable, a good sign for a good wine.

The vineyard was planted in 1991 after the owners, Norm and Ellen Christianson, searched the world for the perfect place to start their wine growing adventure. After several years of trial and perfection, the first Canyon Wind vintage was released in December of 1997. Awards for the Canyon Wind Cellars can be seen around the tasting room, honoring them for their dedication to quality.

TAKE THE TOUR

WHERE TO GO
3907 N. River Road
Palisade, CO 81526

WHEN TO GO
Guided Tour
Tasting Room Hours:
Monday – Saturday
10am – 5pm

DEGREE OF DIFFICULTY
Easy

CONTACT
970.464.0888

www.coloradowinecountry.com/canyonwine

CARLSON VINEYARDS

TAKE THE TOUR

WHERE TO GO
461 35 Road
Palisade, CO 81526

WHEN TO GO
Guided Tour
Daily
11am – 6pm

DEGREE OF DIFFICULTY
Easy

CONTACT
888.464.5554
www.carlsonvineyards.com

A drive out to the Carlson Vineyards will take your mind off any worries. Weaving around the fields of apricots, oranges, apples and grapes, you'll get to the vineyard in a mellow mood.

The vineyard is enormous in size, and it surrounds the tasting room. Grapes can be seen, plump and ripe when close to harvest, filling your eyes with a visual delight.

The owners, Parker and Mary Carlson, have one of the oldest wineries in Colorado, dating to 1988 They've built a reputation of making delicious wines along with their distinctive vineyard image. Parker, the vintner, has received numerous awards for his spirits, and his picture can be seen on many of the Colorado tourism brochures.

Sticking with playful images on the bottle labels, they name their wines interestingly enough. Their most popular wine is Tyrannosaurus Red and the contents of the bottle are 100% Colorado grapes. The first acreage of the vineyard was planted in 1981, in the former apricot orchard, and it continues to grow. The Carlson Vineyards pride themselves on their wines, which are soft and delicious to the palate.

COLORADO CELLARS WINERY

TAKE THE TOUR

WHERE TO GO
3553 E. Road
Palisade, CO 81526

WHEN TO GO
Tasting Room Hours:
Monday – Friday
9am – 4pm
Saturday
Noon – 4

DEGREE OF DIFFICULTY
Easy

CONTACT
970.464.7921
800.848.2812

www.coloradowinecountry.
com/coloradocellars

Founded in 1978, the Colorado Cellars is a family-owned and operated winery. Today, you can visit the exquisite tasting room, which rests upon a hillside overlooking the vineyards and provides a glorious panoramic view of the Grand Valley. The winery also has two gazebo picnic areas and a half-acre grassy knoll located near the tasting room.

Inside the tasting room you'll find 20 varieties of wines, available to take home. Using a fancy tasting system, you are welcome to taste several varieties of wines as you browse the room and view the products and awards. In addition to the Colorado Cellars wine, they produce and offer wines from the Rocky Mountain Vineyards, Orchard Mesa Wine Company, and Colorado Mountain Vinyards.

The winery has a specialty line of products, which are wine-based foods such as salsas, sauces and fudges. Herb wines, made on the premises, are Chardonnay with a variety of herbs such as lemon and pepper.

Colorado Cellar also makes champagne, and since it is the only winery in Colorado to make champagne by hand, there is a large demand for this unique product on a national level.

GRANDE RIVER VINEYARDS

The Grande River Vineyards can be seen from I-70, and they catch the attention of the natives as well as those just traveling through. The winery and vineyard would be an ideal first stop on a wine-tasting tour around Palisade.

The tasting room of the Grande River has a one-of-a-kind cozy European resort feeling. Inside you are able to see the oak barrels, with spirits fermenting inside them, as they rest on the special racks in the room. You will be able to view wine-related items including t-shirts and aprons displayed on the walls.

While standing around a horseshoe-shaped table, you will be able to explore the versatile tastes of the season. The vineyard produces over ten different wines, for which it has won 250 awards. Take a look at the food related items that the vineyard has to offer, as some of the products are quite interesting.

Founding the vineyards in 1987, Stephen Smith planted his first grapes in hopes of offering to Palisade a first-class introduction to the world of wines. The fruits of his labor can be seen behind the building, as the yearling crops have ripened with awesome fruit waiting to be harvested in the fall. The name of the vineyard, Grande River, was chosen to reflect the importance of the Colorado River Valley.

The vineyard has an excellent tour, which covers everything a connoisseur might need to know about their wine. This year it hopes to bottle 5,000 – 7,000 cases of Grande River Barrel Select Chardonnay – an extraordinary feat.

PLUM CREEK CELLARS

In the Plum Creek Cellars parking lot you will be greeted by the official Chardonnay Chicken, who is awaiting your arrival! You will see him, donned in his seven-foot long feathers, in the large picnic area, which is surrounded with grapes in the fields. This is a great location for the Plum Creek Cellars, as the beautiful area provides an elegant atmosphere for their products.

The tasting room has the feeling of a resort cabin. The wines that are available will be displayed on the counters, ready for sampling. There are wine essentials available in the tasting room, including corkscrews and books. Additionally, there are bottles of wine displayed in a fancy stacking system, which shows how delightfully the wine can be presented. The tasting room is big enough to accommodate large groups, and the personal service will make you feel as though you're the only one there.

Plum Creek Cellars is known for its Palisade Red wine. It is a medium wine with the complicated scents of black current, smoky oak, cherries and a hint of mint. This wine is an excellent accompaniment to a chicken dish.

TAKE THE TOUR

WHERE TO GO
3708 G Road
Palisade, CO 81526

WHEN TO GO
Guided Tour
Monday – Saturday
9:30am – 6pm
Best Time for Tour
1 – 4pm

DEGREE OF DIFFICULTY
Easy

CONTACT
970.464.7586
www.coloradowinecountry
.com/plum_creek

ROCKY MOUNTAIN MEADERY

Mead wine, which is made from honey, has been a popular drink since the 16th century. Mead was first produced in old England, and it is believed to have been discovered by the Church, which kept bees for a steady supply of beeswax. Once the wax was separated from the honey, a residue remained. Left to ferment, the residue became a mildly alcoholic drink.

The founders of the Rocky Mountain Meadery, Fred and Connie Strothman, have been making mead since the opening of the facility in 1995. They also own the Confre Cellars, as well as St. Kathryn's Cellar. Mr. Strothman, a retired Federal Administration Law judge, decided to expand his winemaking skills into a serious entrepreneur venture.

The tasting room, better known as The Meading Place, is accompanied by a delightful gift shop. You will have the opportunity to taste the luscious flavors of their four honey wines, which are all named after people from the time of King Arthur. If you are looking for something slightly sweet, the fruit wines blended with honey might be your best choice.

Near the back shop windows, you will have the chance to learn about the wine making process, which can be easily followed as the equipment is neatly arranged.

TAKE THE TOUR

WHERE TO GO
3701 G. Road
Palisade, CO 81526

WHEN TO GO
Tasting Room Hours:
Monday – Saturday
10am – 5pm

DEGREE OF DIFFICULTY
Easy

CONTACT
970.464.7899
www.coloradowinecountry.com
/rocky_mtn_meadery

ST. KATHRYN'S CELLARS

St. Kathryn's Cellars is one of the newest wineries on the Western Slope. It is a small family-owned winery that has been in operation through two generations of the Strothman family. Located next to I-70, the winery overflows with a beauty that can only be found in the Western Slope area. The Grand Mesa can be seen to the east and Mt. Garfield stands behind the winery.

The tasting room is part of a fairly large and popular event center at the winery. The new building has ample parking for the busy summer months and the important events that are held there annually. The winery offers cases of wine, gourmet foods and gifts that will impress you; and a walk through the tasting room will give you a chance to explore the wine accessories that are available. St. Kathryn's Cellars offers a strong selection of variety and fruit wines, which are priced affordably. One of the most popular wines is called Blueberry Bliss, which is a slightly sweet blueberry wine with a refreshing flavor that compliments the simplest of meals.

The winery was named after the winemaker's mother, Kathryn. Her dream was to sit and watch the vineyards grow throughout the seasons. She found this activity perfect for absorbing the sights and sounds near the Grand Mesa. The image on the wine labels is a picture of Kathryn when she was a young woman.

TAKE THE TOUR

WHERE TO GO
888 Elberta Avenue
Palisade, CO 81526

WHEN TO GO
Guided Tour
Monday – Saturday
10am – 5pm
Summer
9am – 7pm

DEGREE OF DIFFICULTY
Easy

CONACT
970.464.9288
www.st-kathryn-cellars.com

BETTY FORD ALPINE GARDENS

If you are looking for a way to relax and take your mind off the stresses of life, head to Vail's Betty Ford Alpine Gardens. This tour is a splendid opportunity to enjoy the beauty of the Rocky Mountains, and to immerse yourself in a unique garden experience.

It begins as you enter through the oversized doors of the main gate, into a high-altitude garden situated 8,200 feet above sea level. There are several distinct gardens on the grounds, each featuring flora that thrive in the Rocky Mountains.

The colorful Mountain Perennial Garden is a large selection of plants grown in the mountains. In this section, alone, you can see more than 1,000 perennial varieties, trees and shrubs. First planted in 1988, the garden has grown outside its perimeters and individual plants can also be seen in the surrounding border.

The Alpine Rock Garden, one of my favorites, has a cascading mountain stream and is the place to marvel at plants native to the high Rocky Mountains. Designers strategically placed benches about the garden to maximize Valley views that you might not otherwise notice. Take the stairway to the top level and glance down at the beautiful grounds and the surrounding mountains. Even in the winter, a walk through the snow-covered area is an extraordinary experience.

The Mountain Meditation Garden is a good place to reflect on life and the beauty of the Rocky Mountains. Here, a wall of Colorado blue spruce trees encloses the garden and its nature within. The gardens were named after Betty Ford, in appreciation for her personal contributions to the Vail area. Next to the gardens is the Gerald Ford Amphitheater, an outdoor venue for all to enjoy.

TAKE THE TOUR

WHERE TO GO
Ford Park
183 Gore Creek Drive
Vail, CO 81657

WHEN TO GO
Self-GuidedTour
Daily
Dawn – Dusk

DEGREE OF DIFFICULTY
Easy

CONTACT
970.476.0103
www.bettyfordalpinegardens.org

Tours FOR FREE™
COLORADO

In the following sections you'll find a variety of events that are free to the public, as well as listings that offer free admission on specified days during the year. There are numerous farmers' markets, community fairs and festivals that are perfect additions to family vacations and outings. These listings will help fill the days with fun places to go and things to see and experience – at no cost.

As with the tours listed in the book, itis best to call in advance to make sure that nothing has changed since press time.

CHATFIELD NATURE PRESERVE

First Friday of every month, 9am - 5pm
8500 Deer Creek Canyon Road, Littleton, CO
303.973.3705
www.botanicgardens.org

Chatfield Nature Preserve is open to the public for free the first Friday of every month.
The Preserve is operated by the Botanic Gardens, but it is located in southwest Denver and is much different from the urban setting of the York Street site. It features nature trails, educational exhibits, a historic farm, a one-room schoolhouse, and working beehives.

DENVER ART MUSEUM

Every Saturday 10am-5pm
13th Avenue and Acoma Street, Denver
720.865.5000
www.denverartmuseum.org

Free general admission every Saturday for Colorado residents. Free general admission every day for kids, 12 and younger.
Half a dozen exhibits are open at a time on rotating schedules. They reflect ancient and modern art, western and international origins, and all forms: textiles, sculpture, photography, paintings, and more.

DENVER BOTANIC GARDENS

Call for specific dates.
1005 York Street, Denver
720.865.3500
www.botanicgardens.org

The Botanic Gardens on York Street has free days monthly from January to October. Visiting the great variety of garden habitats and plant collections at the Botanic Gardens will be as relaxing as it is educational.

DENVER MUSEUM OF NATURE AND SCIENCE

Specified Wednesdays and Sundays, so call ahead
2001 Colorado Boulevard, Denver
303.925.2250
www.dmns.org

In addition to 13 permanent exhibits, the museum features special exhibitions that are presented for a few months at a time. The giant screen IMAX theater is always a big experience, no matter what is playing. The museum is expanding, both in its programs and in its new construction.

DENVER ZOO

FREE DAYS: 2003
Jan 18, Jan 26, Feb 2
Feb 14, Oct 4, Oct 15
Nov 7, Nov 26

23rd Ave. between Colorado Blvd. And York St., Denver
303.376.4800
www.denverzoo.org

Denver's zoo is a fine outing for folks of every age and interest. It features one of the most diverse animal collections in the country. The staff regularly opens new exhibits and keeps the public coming in. Find out when feeding times are and watch the action.

Tours FOR FREE™
COLORADO

Colorado offers numerous annual festivals that are well attended by both vendors and the public. They come in all shapes and sizes, but include everything from food stalls and amusement rides to arts and crafts, free music, local exhibitions, and more. You could spend an hour or an entire weekend milling around and still not see all that awaits you!

As with the tours listed in the book, it is best to call in advance to make sure that nothing has changed since press time.

FREE FESTIVALS

BOULDER CREEK FESTIVAL

FREE Event, Memorial Day Weekend
Along Boulder Creek, From 9th to 14th Streets
Between Arapahoe and Canyon, Boulder, CO
303.449.3825
www.bouldercreekfestival.com

The unique Boulder community presents an Art Show, Fitness and Health events, Earthkeeping, forums, Speakers' Corner, Kids' Place, Rubber Duck Race, live entertainment on multiple stages, gourmet food and all that has contributed for more than a decade to this award-winning festival.

BOULDER CREEK HOMETOWN FAIR & HARVEST FESTIVAL

FREE Event, Labor Day Weekend
Along Boulder Creek, From 9th to 14th Streets
Between Arapahoe and Canyon, Boulder, CO
303.449.3825
www.bouldercreekevents.com/hometown/

The Festival is and end of summer celebration with a small, hometown feel. Enjoy the entertainment, arts and crafts vendors, food court, Chili Cook Off, pie eating contest, and Great Zucchini Races.

BOULDER LIGHTS OF DECEMBER PARADE

FREE Event, Early December, 6 pm
Pearl Street Mall area, Boulder, CO
Call for specific date, 303.449.3774

Boulder community groups present parade entries, and marching groups herald the coming of lights and holiday spirit. Santa Clause makes an appearance.

BRIGHTON, CULTUREFEST... TASTE OF BRIGHTON

2nd Saturday in June, Brighton, CO
303.655.2217
www.ci.brighton.co.us

Demonstrations, multi-cultural entertainment, crafts, and food highlight this celebration of the culture and business life of Brighton.

BRIGHTON, FESTIVAL OF LIGHTS

Mid-December, Main Street to City Hall, Brighton, Brighton
Call for specific date, 303.655.2217

Before the parade begins, there will be a Winter Festival from 4 to 6 pm at City Hall featuring live music and kids' activities. The parade begins at 5:30pm at Denver and Main Streets and continues down Main. Dress warmly and enjoy this big event attended by thousands.

CHERRY CREEK ARTS FESTIVAL

July, Denver, CO
Call for specific dates, 303.355.2787
www.cherryarts.org

The Cherry Creek community presents this outdoor juried arts festival, which encourages visitors to meet and talk to the artists, sample fine cooking, and even create some art themselves.

CINCO DE MAYO FESTIVAL

May, Civic Center Park, Denver, CO
303.534.8342 x122
www.newsed.org

May 5 is the date of a historical victory of Mexican peasants over French invaders. The festival celebrates the event with folkloric dance, storytelling, a parade, foods, arts and crafts, and the sounds of salsa, mariachi, and border music

DOWNTOWN BOULDER FALL FESTIVAL

FREE Festival, Late September
Pearl Street Mall, Boulder, CO
Call for specific dates, 303.449.3774
www.boulderdowntown.com/

This three-day festival turns Pearl Street Mall into Octoberfest with international and local musicians, tents and booths serving food and microbrews from around the world, and an arts show. The kids will like the amusement rides.

FESTIVAL OF MOUNTAIN & PLAIN /TASTE OF COLORADO

Labor Day weekend
Civic Center Park,Denver, CO
303.295.6330
www.downtowndenver.com/evt_toc.htm

This festival is a huge four-day, outdoor, food and entertainment event. It offers a chance to experience some of the outstanding artistic, musical, and cultural talents of Coloradoans.

INTERNATIONAL BUSKERFEST

June, 16th Street Mall, Denver, CO
Call for specific free dates, 303.295.1195
www.downtowndenver.com

Notable street artists will amuse and amaze you: jugglers, acrobats, magicians, fire-eaters, comedians, and other specialty entertainers – all known as buskers.

PARADE OF LIGHTS

December
Denver, CO
Call for specific dates.
303.295.6330
www.downtowndenver.com/evt_pol.htm

Downtown Denver's nighttime skyline is part of the show for this annual holiday parade. Giant balloons, marching bands, and floats blazing with lights make this an impressive event.

PEOPLES FAIR

Early June
Civic Center Park, Denver, CO 303.8301651
See the website for specific dates.
www.peoplesfair.com

Celebrating Capitol Hill's diverse cultural heritage and neighborhood pride, this event features live entertainment, family fun, and a great variety of arts and crafts exhibits. Volunteers put the fair together, and community projects receive funds from it.

CINCO DE MAYO/SEMANA LATINA

Late April – early May
Island Grove Community Park Greeley, CO
Call for specific dates, 970.350.9451

The spirit of Mexico lives in the fine arts, crafts, music, and foods of this event. A car show, sports competition, and kids' carnival means there's something for everyone.

FESTIVAL OF TREES

Late November-Early December
Union Colony Civic Center, Greeley, CO
Call for specific dates, 970.350.9451

Traditional Christmas singing and music add to the spectacle of decorated holiday trees and wreaths. Children can make holiday crafts projects, and families can watch classic Christmas movies.

SOUTHEAST

COLORADO FAIR PARADE

First Saturday of August
Pueblo, CO
See the website for specific dates.
800.876.4567
www.coloradosfair.com

Part of the celebration of the Colorado State Fair is the grand parade that starts from Union and D Street at 10am. The parade's theme shows itself in creative floats and a variety of highlights. The Governor and other dignitaries will be there, along with marching bands and beautiful horses. This is the biggest but not the only parade that complements the State Fair.

BUENA VISTA, GOLD RUSH DAYS

Early August
Buena Vista, CO 719.395.6612
See the website for specific dates.
www.fourteenernet.com/goldrush/

Gold Rush days come to life again with a championship pack burro race, Western and square dancing, melodrama, gold panning, mock gunfights, and over 120 booths with food and craft items.

CARBONDALE MOUNTAIN FAIR

Lasr Full Weekend in July
Carbondale, CO
Call for specific dates, 970.963.1680
www.carbondalearts.com

Enjoy the mountain air at the peak of the summer in Carbondale. Take in the arts and crafts, international food, live entertainment, children's and adults' fun activities of the fair.

ESTES PARK, CATCH THE GLOW CHRISTMAS PARADE

Day after Thanksgiving, 5:30pm
Estes Park, CO
800.443.7837
www.estesparkresort.com

This mountain community presents a Christmas parade of lights including storybook figures, floats, and marching bands. Thousands of people come to see this special event, so come early and spend the day in beautiful Estes Park

VAIL ARTS FESTIVAL

June
Vail, CO
Call for specific dates, 866.750.4055

Live entertainment complements this juried arts festival in the mountain resort town of Vail. The annual event is a chance to see fine work in painting, photography, woodcarving, stained glass, pottery, and more.

PALISADE PEACH FESTIVAL

Third Weekend of August
Palisade Park, 8th and Main
Palisade, CO 970.464.7458
See the web site for specific dates.
www.palisadepeachfest.com/

People come from great distances to taste the peaches from this region. A peach recipe contest is a main event, and there is a peach-eating contest for any who dare. Palisade puts on a fine event with a parade, a band concert, food booths, and arts and crafts.

Tours FOR FREE™
COLORADO

County Fairs are lots of fun for the entire family. For kids there's often a carnival, petting zoo, and other activities. Adults enjoy the various animal and agricultural exhibitions, as well as a wide array of food stalls featuring local specialties such as turkey legs and deep-fried onion rings. Most counties in Colorado host free fairs during the summer months.

As with the tours listed in the book, it is best to call in advance to make sure that nothing has changed since press time.

ADAMS COUNTY FAIR

July 30 - August 3
Brighton/ Henderson Adams County Fairgrounds
Contact: Carol Moon 303.637.8007

ARAPAHOE COUNTY 4-H COMPLETION EVENTS

July
Various Locations
Contact: Gail Loeffler 303.730.1920

ARCHULETA COUNTY FAIR

July 31 – August 3
344 Highway 84, Pagosa Springs, CO
Contact: Emzy Baker 970.264.5931

BACA COUNTY FAIR

August 4 – 9
28500 County Road 24 6/10, Springfield, CO
Contact: 719.523.6933

BENT COUNTY FAIR

July 19 – 26
1499 Ambassador Thompson Boulevard, Las Animas, CO
Contact: John Ming 719.456.0764

BENT COUNTY HARVEST SHOW

October 7 – 9
1499 Ambassador Thompson Boulevard , Las Animas, CO
Contact: 719.456.0764

BOULDER COUNTY FAIR AND LIVESTOCK SHOW

August
9595 Nelson Road, Longmont, CO
Contact: Kathy Lynch 303.772.7170

CHAFFEE, NEW-OLD FASHIONED CHAFFEE COUNTY FAIR

10165 County Road 120, Salida, CO
Contact: Dick Scherbarth 719.539.6151
July – August

CHEYENNE COUNTY FAIR

Cheyenne Wells Fairgrounds, 425 S. 7th West
Contact: Gary McNeely 719.767.5716
August

COUNTY DAYS ORDWAY

Ordway, CO
Contact: Ron Ackerman 719.267.4741, ext. 7
July

CUSTER COUNTY FAIR

N. Highway 69, Westcliffe, CO
Contact: Beverly Goertz 719.783.2514
July 16 – 20

DELTA COUNTY FAIR

Hotchkiss, CO
Contact: Robbie Baird LaValley 970.874.2195
August

DOLORES COUNTY FAIR

1/ 4 mile north of County Road 2; 4 miles west of Dove Creek on Highway 666
Dove Creek, CO
Contact: Dan Fernandez 970.677.2283
August 8 – 11

DOUGLAS COUNTY FAIR

Douglas County Fairgrounds, Castle Rock, CO
Contact: Kayedeane Miller 720.733.6941
August

EAGLE COUNTY FAIR

July 26 – August 3
1400 Fairgrounds Road, Eagle, CO
Contact: Dick Kesler 800.611.1378

ELBERT COUNTY FAIR

July 27 – August 4
Elbert County Fairgrounds, Simla, CO
Contact: 303.621.3162

EL PASO COUNTY FAIR

July 20 – 28
366 10th Street, Calahan, CO
Contact: Jim Abendeschan 719.520.7881

FREMONT COUNTY FAIR

July 26 – August 3
Canon City, Royal Gorge Rodeo Grounds, S. 9th Street, Canon City, CO
Contact: 719.275.6722

GARFIELD COUNTY FAIR

Garfield County Fairgrounds
Contact: Toni Penton 970.625.2514
August 7 – 10

GUNNISON COUNTY CATTLEMEN'S DAYS

July 11 – 20
Gunnison, CO
Contact: Kim Fabrizius 970.641.1260

HOLLY GATEWAY

September 26 – 29
Holly, CO
Contact: Nancy Shaffer 719.336.7734 or 719.537.6215

HUERFANO COUNTY 4-H FAIR

August 6 – 10
Huerfano County Fairgrounds, Walsenburg, CO
Contact: Albert Anselmo 719.738.3329

JEFFCO FAIR

July 30 – August 3
Golden-Jefferson County Fairgrounds, Golden, CO
Contact: Alexa Lamm or Megan Tifft 303.271.6620

KIOWA COUNTY FAIR

September 10 – 14
15001 Highway 287, Eads, CO
Contact: Pam Weirch or Bruce Fickenscher 719.438.5321

KIT CARSON COUNTY FAIR

August 4 – 9
Kit Carson County Fairgrounds
Burlington, CO
Contact: Bette Bailly or John Nichols 719.346.5566 or 719.346.0111

KREMMLING, MIDDLE PARK FAIR

September 18 – 22
210 11th Street, Kremmling, CO
Contact: Chris Scott 970.724.3436

LA PLATA COUNTY FAIR

August 6 – 10
La Plata County Fairgrounds, Durango, CO
Contact: Randy McKee 970.259.3158

LARIMER COUNTY FAIR

July 25 – August 6
Larimer County Fairgrounds, Loveland, CO
Contact: 970.669.6760

LAS ANIMAS COUNTY FAIR

August – September
Trinidad, Fairgrounds, 2200 N. Linden Avenue, Trinidad, CO
Contact: Dean Oatman 719.846.6681

LINCOLN COUNTY FAIR

Lincoln County Fairgrounds, Hugo, CO
Contact: Mike Mosher 719.743.2606
August 4 – 9

LOGAN COUNTY FAIR

August
1120 Pawnee, Sterling, CO
Contact: Les Baney 970.522.0888

MESA COUNTY FAIR

July
2785 Highway 50, Grand Junction, CO
Contact: Marilyn Calhount 970.858.9328

MOFFAT COUNTY FAIR COUNTY

August 1 – 9
Highway 40 East, County Roadaig, CO
Contact: Pat Morales 970.824.3476

MONTEZUMA COUNTY FAIR

July 31 – August 2
10300 Highway 160, Cortez, CO
Contact: Jan Sennhenn 970.565.3123

MONTROSE COUNTY FAIR

July
1001 N. 2nd Street, Montrose, CO
Contact: Dave McManus 970.249.3935

MORGAN COUNTY FAIR

August 2 – 7
750 Ellsworth, Fort Morgan, CO
Contact: Marlin Eisenach 970.867.2493

NORTH PARK FAIR

September 5 – 7
Walden, Wattenberg Community Center, Walden, CO
Contact: Brenda Brown or Stanley Gollobith 970.723.4298

OTERO, ARKANSAS VALLEY FAIR

August 19 – 24
800 N. 9th Street, Rocky Ford, CO
Contact: Sally Cope 719.254.7215

OURAY COUNTY FAIR

August 29 - September 1
Ouray County Fairgrounds, Montrose, CO
Contact: Dave McManus 970.249.3935

PARK COUNTY, PARK CITY FAIR

July 12 – 20
880 Bogue Street, Fairplay, CO
Contact: Deb Oakes 303.838.6230

PHILLIPS COUNTY FAIR

July
Phillips County Fairgrounds, Holyoke, CO
Contact: Bonnie Sherman 970.854.3616

PROWERS, SAND & SAGE ROUND-UP

August
Prowers County Fairground
Lamar, CO
Contact: Nancy Shaffer 719.336.7734

PUEBLO COUNTY FAIR

July
Colorado State Fairgrounds, Pueblo, CO
Contact: Bernard Elliott 719.583.6566

RIO BLANCO COUNTY FAIR

July – August
Rio Blanco County Fairgrounds, Meeker, CO
Contact: Bill Ekstrom 970.878.4093

ROUTT COUNTY FAIR

August 9 – 17
365 S. Poplar Street, Hayden, CO
Contact: Terry Doherty 970.276.3068 or 970.879.0825

SAN LUIS VALLEY FAIR

July 23 – August 6
Ski Hi Park, Sanford, CO
Contact: Adele Barr 719.274.4204

SAN MIGUEL BASIN FAIR

July
1130 Summit Street, San Miguel, CO
Contact: Paul Finley 970.327.0300 or 970.327.4393

SEDGWICK COUNTY FAIR

July 31 – August 3
Sedgwick County Fairgrounds, Julesburg, CO
Contact: Jim Beck 970.474.2448 or 970.474.3479

SUMMIT, MOUNTAIN COMMUNITY FAIR

July 10 – 13
Silverthorne Arena, Blue River Park, Silverthorne, CO
Contact: Moe Schultz 970.513.8081

TELLER COUNTY FAIR

August
510 Golden Street, County Roadipple County Roadeek, CO
Contact: Carlton Brown 719.689.2295

WASHINGTON, EASTERN COLORADO ROUND-UP

East 2nd Street, Akron, CO
Contact: Dave Jones 970.345.2287 or 970.345.2565

WELD COUNTY FAIR

July 19 – 28
Island Grove Park, Greeley, CO
Contact: Sandi Meier 970.356.4000, ext. 4485

YUMA COUNTY FAIR

August 3 – 7
Yuma County Fairgrounds, W. Hoag Avenue, Yuma, CO
Contact: Ed Berry 970.848.2291 or 970.358.4365

Tours
FOR FREE™
COLORADO

Farmers markets are a great resource for finding fresh produce and vegetables, as well as flowers and organic foods. Strolling along, looking at all the homegrown goods artfully displayed in stalls or right off the backs of trucks is also a pleasant way to spend a morning. What's better is that prices are usually below market rates, as farmers can sell directly to the public, avoiding any commissions added by a retailer. Vendors are friendly, and are always eager to share what they know about agriculture and their products. Most cities in Colorado feature farmers markets, usually on a weekend morning and often on a weekday during summer to early fall. Some markets offer arts and crafts shows during peak months, as well. Go once or go often, as produce changes regularly with the season, making for a new experience with each visit.

ARVADA FARMERS MARKET

June – September: Thursday, 9am – 2pm
5590 Olde Wadsworth Boulevard, Arvada, CO

AURORA FARMERS MARKET I

June – October: Tuesday, 11am
June – October: Saturday, 7am
Buckingham Square Shopping Center, Aurora, CO 80010
Contact: Pam Wilson 303.361.6169
Email: Daurorabus@aol.com

AURORA FARMERS MARKET II

June – October: Tuesday, 11am
June – October: Saturday, 7am
9750 East Colfax Avenue, Aurora, CO 80010
Contact: Pam Wilson 303.361.6169
Email: Daurorabus@aol.com

AURORA SOUTH FARMERS MARKET II

June – October: Wednesday, 7am
15324 East Hampden Circle, Aurora, CO 80013
Contact: Pam Wilson 303.361.6169
Email: Daurorabus@aol.com

BOULDER COUNTY FARMERS MARKET

May – October: Wednesday, 10am – 2pm.
April – November: Saturday, 8 am – 2 pm
13th Street between Arapahoe Avenue & Canyon Boulevard
Boulder, CO 80308
Contact: Jim "JT" Taylor 303.910.2236
Email: info@boulderfarmers.org
www.boulderfarmers.org

CANON CITY FARMERS MARKET

June – October: Wednesday, 7:30am – 1pm
Holy Cross Abbey U.S. Highway 50, Canon City, CO 81226
Contact: Kris Ray 719.275.1514
Email: fremont@coop.ext.colostate.edu

CASTLE ROCK FARMERS MARKET

July – September: Saturday, 8am – Noon
Human Services Building parking lot, Castle Rock, CO 80104
Contact: Michelle Wach 303.660.7312
Email: douglas@coop.ext.colostate.edu

CHERRY CREEK FARMERS MARKET

June – September: Wednesday, 9am – 1pm
May 6 – October 28: Saturday, 7:30am – 12:30pm
Bed, Bath & Beyond parking lot, 1st Avenue & University, Cherry Creek, CO 80202
Contact: Chris Webster 303.449.1982

COLLBRAN FARMERS MARKET

May – September: Saturday, 9am – Noon
202 Main, Collbran, CO

COLORADO SPRINGS FARMERS MARKET I

Mid June – Mid October: Monday, 7am – 1:30pm
Acacia Park on Bijou & Nevada Streets, Colorado Springs, CO 80903
Contact: Betty Mull 719.598.4215

COLORADO SPRINGS FARMERS MARKET II

Mid June – Mid October: Saturday, 7am – 1:30pm
24th Street & W. Colorado Avenue, Colorado Springs, CO 80903
Contact: Betty Mull 719.598.4215

COLORADO SPRINGS FARMERS MARKET III

July – Early October: Thursday, 7am – 1:30pm
Memorial Park, East Pikes Peak Avenue & Union Boulevard
Colorado Springs, CO 80903
Contact: Betty Mull 719.598.4215

COLORADO SPRINGS FARMERS MARKET IV

Mid June – September: Friday, 7am – 1pm
5225 East Platte Avenue, Colorado Springs, CO 80903
Contact: Betty Mull 719.598.4215

COLORADO SPRINGS FARMERS MARKET V

4515 Barnes Road, Colorado Springs, CO 80903
Mid June – Mid October: Saturday, 7am – 1:30pm

CORTEZ FARMERS MARKET I

25 North Market Street, Cortez, CO 81321
Contact: Debbie White 970.565.1151
June – October: Saturday, 8am – Noon

CORTEZ FARMERS MARKET II

Late July – November: Saturday, 6am
Montezuma County Courthouse, 109 West Main Street, Cortez, CO 81321
Contact: Debbie White 970.565.1151

DENVER FARMERS MARKET

June – October: Saturday, 7am
June 4 – September 24: Sunday, 9am – 1pm
City Park Esplande, Between 17th & Colfax, Denver, CO 80202
Contact: Shannon McCurry 303.254.8451

DILLON FARMERS MARKET

June – September: 9am – 1pm
Marina Park parking lot, Dillon, CO

DURANGO FARMERS MARKET

June – October: Saturday, 8am – 1pm
1st National Bank parking lot, 259 W. 9th Street, Durango, CO 81302
Contact: Carol Clark 970.259.9339

ESTES PARK FARMERS MARKET

June – September: Thursday, 8am – 1pm
2200 Mall Road, Estes, CO

EVERGREEN FARMERS MARKET

June – October: Tuesday, 10am – 3pm
Evergreen Wal-Mart parking lot, Evergreen, CO

FT. COLLINS FARMERS MARKET I

July – September: Saturday, 8am – Noon
Larimer County Courthouse parking lot; Corner of Mountain & Mason Streets
Ft. Collins, CO 80524
Contact: Kiri Saftler 970.493.1427

FT. COLLINS FARMERS MARKET II

June – September: Sunday, 9am – 1pm
June – September: Wednesday, 2pm – 6pm
Steele's Market parking lot , 802 West Drake, Ft. Collins, CO 80524
Contact: Kiri Saftler 970.493.1427

GLENWOOD SPRINGS FARMERS MARKET

July – October: Saturday, 8am – 3:30pm
True Value/Van Rand Shopping Center, Glenwood Springs, CO 81652
Contact: Ken Kuhns, Jr., 970.876.2850

GRAND JUNCTION FARMERS MARKET I

Mid April – Mid to late November: Wednesday & Saturday, 7am – Noon
Teller Arms Shopping Center, 2401 North Avenue, Grand Junction, CO 81501
Contact: Jo Ann Gobbo 970.243.2446

GRAND JUNCTION FARMERS MARKET II

July – October: Monday & Friday, 7am – Noon
1st and Colorado, Grand Junction, CO 81501
Contact: Jo Ann Gobbo 970.243.2446

GREELEY FARMERS MARKET

June – October: Wednesday, 4pm – 6pm
June – October: Saturday, 7:30am – 11am
902 7th Avenue, Greeley, CO 80631
Contact: Karen Scopel 970.350.9783

LAKEWOOD, VILLA ITALIA MALL

June – October: Thursday, 11am
W. Alameda & Wadsworth, Lakewood, CO

LITTLETON, SQUARE PLAZA SHOPPING CENTER I

June – September: Thursday, 9am – 1pm
Wadsworth & Bowles, Littleton, CO

LITTLETON, SQUARE PLAZA SHOPPING CENTER II

June – October: Wednesday, 11am
Broadridge Plaza Shopping Center Broadway & Ridge Road, Littleton, CO

LONGMONT FARMERS MARKET

July – September: Monday & Tuesday, 3 – 6pm
June – October: Saturday, 8am – 1pm
Northwest corner of Boulder County Fairgrounds, Hover Road & Boston Avenue
Longmont, CO 80501
Contact: Laura Korth 970.532.0434

LOUISVILLE FARMERS MARKET

June – September: 9am – 2pm
908 Main Street, Louisville, CO

LOVELAND FARMERS MARKET

Tuesday, 2pm – 6pm
Corner of Lincoln & 5th Street
July – Late October

MONTROSE FARMERS MARKET

April – October: Wednesday & Saturday, 8:30am – 1pm
2.2 blocks north on Stough off Main Street, Montrose, CO 81401
Contact: Jeanne Austin 303.249.9725

NORTHGLENN MARKET PLACE

June – October: Friday 7am
104th & I-25, North end of Melody Drive by Marshalls, Northglenn, CO

PUEBLO FARMERS MARKET I

July – October: 7am – 1pm
July – October: Friday, 7am – 1pm
Midtown Shopping Center, W. 6th Street, Pueblo, CO 81001
Contact: Market Secretary 719.583.6566

RIDGWAY FARMERS MARKET

June – September: Sundays, 8am – 1pm
July – October: Friday, 7am – 1pm
Ouray County Fairgrounds, Intersection, Highways 550 & 62
Ridgway, CO 81001
Contact: Jane Bennett 970.626.9775
Email: jbennett@co.ouray.co.us

SALIDA FARMERS MARKET

July – August: Monday, 7am – 2pm
Alpine Park, 4th & F Street

STERLING FARMERS MARKET

July 15 – Late September: Tuesday, 5:30pm & Saturday, 8am
Southeast corner of Wal-Mart parking lot, Sterling, CO

WESTMINSTER FARMERS MARKET

Early June – Late October: Sunday, 10am
94th & Sheridan, Westminster, CO

WOODLAND PARK FARMERS MARKET

June – September: Friday, 7am – 1pm
Kavanaugh Field, Woodland Park, CO 80863

COLORADO

INDEX

TOURS BY NAME

AGRICULTURE

BREWERIES

TOTALLY COLORADO

After twelve years as a literary agent, Jodi Jill has moved on to being a full time author. Tours For Free Colorado comes from her love of Colorado, touring and figuring out how to get the most out of a buck! She is the creator to the Quit Whining and Read! Literacy program where she promotes literacy through art, information and making donations to literacy programs. The QuitWhining.com website and her monthly newsletter "Make Words Work" has become an important part of promoting and encouraging literacy. Jill is the author of five other books, including the popular Postmark Loveland and anthologies of her nationally syndicated puzzle Brain Baffler. Her love of puzzles led to her founding National Puzzle day, which is celebrated every January.

NOTES/TRAVEL LOG

NOTES/TRAVEL LOG

NOTES/TRAVEL LOG

NOTES/TRAVEL LOG

FREE TOURS
GO!

Grab the guidebook that gets you there for FREE

Tours For Free books are packed full of fun, entertaining, and educational tours.

From Candy Factories to wineries, newspapers to dinosaur tracks, guitars to golf clubs, these handy guides have something for everyone.

Whether you are traveling or if you live in the region – the Tours For Free books are a must have.

- A fantastic way to stretch your vacation dollar
- Perfect for entertaining visitors from out of town
- Ideal for weekend trips that don't cost a dime
- Wonderful for finding things to entertain the kids during the summer

TOUR FREE IN:

Colorado
Southern California & Las Vegas
Northern California
New York
Illinois

WWW.TOURSFORFREE.COM